BECOME A GREAT LEADER AND COACH USING NLP
by
Steve Kay
ISBN: 978-1-9999129-8-7

Published by

i2i Publishing. Manchester.
www.i2ipublishing.co.uk

For Dawn and Josh

Introduction

Let's start with something controversial. Your job as a leader is NOT to inspire other people. I believe it's much more profound than that.

Your job as a leader is to *be* inspired. And I will show you how.

By being inspired, you will enable other people to inspire *themselves* through your new and improved approach to leadership and coaching.

You may be questioning whether people can actually inspire themselves? This is unsurprising, traditional management training argues that people are passive in the inspiration process and have to be inspired by something external, usually their manager.

But I would argue that anyone can have an "aha!" moment, if they realise it is their choice to feel stimulated, motivated and energised to take action. In other words, you have to *decide* to be inspired. But, don't worry, it is fairly easy to do and simply involves re-educating yourself.

You already have the capability to inspire yourself. You learned to walk and talk, to laugh and have fun, and, most importantly, to ask questions. Curiosity is essential, but you probably asked more questions when you were two than you have in the last ten years, it is essential to revive this inquisitiveness.

You already have all you need inside of you to become a great leader. I'll just provide a few insights to enable you to discover your own unique abilities to help you become a better you.

Think about this for a moment. You enter a darkened room and press the light switch, the current flows and then, voila, the room brightens. You don't provide the energy or the electricity, it is already in the wiring. All you do is click the switch and the room lights up.

This book is about flicking on the switch in others so that they can harness the energy they already possess and light up their career and life. You too have potential energy waiting to be untapped. Are you ready to have the lights switched on?

In order to be a great leader or coach, you have to be an awe-inspiring version of yourself, that way you can be a role model for others and get the most satisfaction from your vocation or career. I say vocation as being a great leader is much more than doing a job. It provides a purpose, or, as Simon Sinek describes it, a *why*.

Recently, I was at my Uncle Kevin's funeral. The Priest told the congregation about how Kevin did his job as a bricklayer with pride, and recounted the tale of how, in one bad winter, Kevin lit a stove near the building materials to keep them dry. Worried that the fire would burn out, Kevin got out of bed at midnight and drove back to the site to rekindle the stove, in fact, he did this every night for a week! Whatever your job, doing that little bit more and having a purpose will differentiate you from the norm.

There are hundreds of books on leadership and coaching. Lots of the leadership books contain 'big' words that are aimed at academia and written by people who have never worked in an office, factory or hospital.

I will demonstrate to you that leadership is not about big words or complex theories. It is, in fact, a process of turning on someone's lights, then showing them where the switch is so that they can do it for themselves!

Although fewer books are written on the use of Neuro Linguistic Programming specifically, I was still disappointed to find that the language used by some authors was very complex, making it difficult to grasp. It seemed to be written with the intention of making it appear scientific, possibly to increase its credibility. My aim is to clarify and simplify some of the jargon, and blend the concepts of NLP into leadership and coaching, to bring you a no-nonsense guide full of useful tips that you can use straight away.

Before writing this book, I thought I'd review the work of a few successful writers, their writing style and their humour. I deliberately chose authors who were not in the business of personal development.

I had always admired the articles that Jeremy Clarkson wrote for *The Sunday Times*, and, one day, I picked up his new book at the airport, only to discover that the whole book, all £8.99 of it, was compiled of his old newspaper articles! I felt a bit cheated, having read many of them before. However, it gave me an idea!

I have been writing blogs for our company newsletter for years, so I thought I would include a few along the way for you to enjoy, allowing you to look at the topic from a different angle. By the time you read these blogs one or two of the characters may have gone to a better place, but the message is still very relevant.

Now, you might think that you are not a leader, you don't manage a team and you are not a coach. So, is this book still for you? Yes, absolutely, this book is for anyone who wants to improve themselves, have a greater impact on their organisation and those around them.

Chapter One — Don't Be a Norm

Imagine that you discover a time machine behind the stationery cupboard. You and your colleagues climb inside. It's dark, and a bit musty. There is a whiz and a judder and, before you know it, you are hurtling back through the decades, to a time when the punk movement was being born.

You land in the year of 1976, in a factory situated on the site of your current place of work. Outside, in the car park, in designated spots, there is a row of British Leyland Austin Marinas, painted in a light brown colour, and two Rovers belonging to the big cheeses.

You walk through the offices and into a factory producing pressings and machining components. A strange figure greets you. He is wearing a light grey suit with a gravy stain on his rather greasy tie. He introduces himself as Norman, the foreman of the factory. He has a Player's No. 6 fag resting on his lower lip and black, Brylcreemed hair combed back from his forehead. Norman has long given up any realistic hope of achieving company car status, although, each morning, he admires his factory manager's turd-coloured Marina. The truth is, Norman feels that *he* deserves the car after 25 years loyalty to the company!

"Time for a cuppa," you hear him mutter, as he wanders off to the canteen.

"Norm," one of his men calls after him, "we're late with the GEC order."

"No worries, Bob." Norm replies. "They can wait a few days, buggers were on strike again last week."

1

You get back into the time machine and set the date for 1996. The building has been transformed. People are working at desks with computers, entering data and writing their own reports. Emails are just beginning to transform the work place. You notice it is after six o'clock, yet there are still people in the office beavering away, dressed smartly in business suits. You are witnessing the birth of presentism and busy-ness. As they leave, some get into their company Ford Mondeos and others into their personal cars, many are carrying briefcases and laptop bags home with them.

The 'Normans' have all but disappeared, or have they? One of your colleagues comments on the herd behaviour. She has noticed.

Finally, your last stop is just ten years ago. The old building has been demolished, manufacturing has been offshored. A new suite of offices stands in its place. There are people gathering in open spaces, talking loudly into their mobile phones as they eye their new BMW. They could have chosen the Ford again, but they want to show that they are going places.

Your colleague pauses as you exit the time machine.

"Fascinating," she exclaims.

"What is?" Another colleague inquires.

"Well," she responds, "it's like in maths, do you remember the bell curve and how it is a pattern in nature for everything to fall around the average?"

Your other colleague looks at his feet and mutters about standard deviations and three-sigma. It is all too much, he had just scraped through maths!

"That's right," she replies, "you can plot the workers in a bell curve and it would reveal a normal distribution, with only 4 or 5% of people in the top or bottom of the range and, obviously, you don't want to be at the bottom! What I have observed is that the average or mean has moved since the 1970s. People are working harder and smarter, and competition is fierce, but most of them still have the herd mentality. Norman lives on, but he has evolved!"

"So, what is the answer?" the other colleague asked.

"Hmm, I suppose we have to be a little bit different from the norm," she mused, "and make sure we are in the top 2 or 3%!"

I was once a Norm, for quite a long time actually, and, speaking as a former norm, I would like you to consider this.

If you are in your early twenties, being forty seems like a long way off, but time will fly by. Not necessarily the days and weeks, they may drag, but the years will. If you are in a job that does not give you a buzz, and you feel that there is something missing, you have a choice:

Option 1

Accept your lot and become one of the norms. Norms are 'normal' people who are good at what they do, but there are quite a lot of them around, some company directors and senior civil servants are norms. Even prime ministers can be norms (not Winston Churchill though). There are so many, in fact, that norms represent most of middle and senior management. They often went to a good school, have a goodish (middle-class) job, they do okay, they probably have nice friends and live in a nice house. They could even be a successful scientist or engineer, a writer or a TV presenter!

It is not necessarily what you do for a living, but *how* you go about it. A typical norm may get a bit bored from time to time, but it's comfy. A norm will read this book, but not do anything with it.

Option 2

Alternatively, you could start, from today, being your very best. Living life with a spring in your step. Supporting, coaching and encouraging people around you. Doing everything to the best of your ability and taking responsibility for what happens in your life.

Let's explore option 2. We are surrounded by norms; the type of people who operate mostly on autopilot, rarely leaving their comfort zones. Whatever your role, I'm suggesting that you can shine from the inside-out. Rather than seeing what you can gain for yourself, start with what you can give. It only takes little steps to be more than average; a friendly smile, a cheerful disposition and performing at your very best. It means running a meeting and starting the agenda with positive results and team success stories. It means acknowledging problems, but focusing everyone on coming up with solutions.

If you want a promotion, then it is no good saying to your manager, "just give me the promotion, boss. Then you'll see what I can really do."

The natural law of life seems to be that what you put in, you get out. Norms tend to wait for the good stuff, whilst being mediocre to good. However, this concept is *not* just about promotion, it is about being better than average, or the norm, whatever you do in life.

According to Earl Nightingale, many countries and organisations are geared to the lowest common denominator. He used an analogy of a convoy of ships during the Second World War, which sailed in formation to gain maximum protection from enemy submarines; the convoy could only sail at the speed of the slowest vessel.

Fast forward to the present day and Kim Cameron, author of *Positive Leadership,* suggests that, "for the most part, organisations are designed to foster stability, steadiness and predictability, that is, to remain in the middle of the continuum." He argues that organisations with positive leadership create a "positive deviance", which results in success. Of course, some organisations create "negative deviance", which results in stress, illness and unprofitability.

In traffic where speed is restricted to 50 miles per hour you can only go as fast as the car in front of you, even if you are in a Porsche. The same applies in many organisations, people are held up by procedures and routine working patterns that restrict creativity and effectiveness. There are still too many managers who are transactional, focusing on the bottom line and their key performance indicators and not enough on their people. KPIs are important, but these managers are sometimes missing the big picture and not appreciating the potential of the individuals around them, who could be encouraged and coached to expand their capabilities and engagement.

Chapter Two — How to Be a Better You

Okay, you have decided you don't want to be a norm, that is the very first step. However, every day you will have to remind yourself of your decision until you develop new habits. But don't worry, this is not like a weight loss programme where you can't eat chocolate or drink beer. Actually, it will be quite painless, all you have to do is follow some simple steps to re-programme your thinking.

You have already been your awesome self many times. Can you remember a moment when you felt really motivated and full of energy, with the attitude that you could do anything? When you felt like that, did you discover that you were being more effective and achieving results beyond your usual norm?

There are a few simple techniques you can learn in order to achieve that great feeling more often and, after a time, they will become natural habits.

Let's start by explaining neuro linguistic programming (NLP) — what does it mean and what are the fundamentals? Breaking down the acronym, *neuro* relates to the brain, *linguistic* is the language we use to others and our self-talk, and *programming* is all about the unconscious habits or patterns of learned behaviour that run our lives. A good example is driving a car, we don't consciously think about dipping the clutch to change gear. NLP provides you with a greater understanding of the world around you, enabling you to see events and people in a different light. NLP is about making changes from the inside, to your habits, beliefs and behaviours, to make you a more effective person. It is like a user manual for your brain, rather like a smartphone with a whole host of apps, some of which you may already possess, but have not opened yet, and some of which can be downloaded. NLP is like a software upgrade for your brain, but it will only work if you make changes to your thinking and self-talk.

Personal Leadership — How to Discover Your Inner Blueprint for Enjoyment

It was a beautiful, sunny (but cold) February day right in the middle of half term. My 12-year-old son had asked me earlier in the morning if I fancied a kick around with him. This is something I'd got out of the habit of doing, these days he did it with his mates. Without realising I was doing it I fobbed him off with the classic, "Maybe later, Josh, after I've finished this?"

I was working on an activity for a senior leadership conference. It was based on the norm concept, and what actions people could take to become inspired and have a positive impact on their teams. I was getting very excited by this, as I anticipated a room buzzing with energy.

And then, it dawned on me! The fob-off from earlier had been the norm version of me, who didn't fancy a game of footy with my lad, but the best version of me most certainly did.

Josh and I spent an hour outside getting gloriously muddy doing cross bar challenges. It was the best hour of the day and yet so simple. It occurred to me that you don't have to do much to be your best self and have fun.

So, I have explained what NLP is, now we'll take a look at how it works and what to do, starting with the process of reading a book. When you read the words on the page, you picture the scenes and characters in your mind, you hear the voices of those characters and become deeply engrossed in the story, gripped by the tension of the plot. If it is a happy tale you smile and feel good. So, words trigger pictures, and these trigger feelings. It is the same with the words you use to yourself or what others say to you. If you use positive words to yourself, they are just good thoughts; the feelings generated will have a positive influence on your behaviour and attitude toward the world around you. Simply put, what goes into your mind and what you think about can become a seedbed for positive results or infertile land that produces mediocrity.

Let's explore how your mind functions. Get ready for a life-changing journey through the operations centre of your mind and the way you perceive the world around you. You are about to experience a new and more exciting future.

The diagram below is a simple picture of what is happening in our mind and how what we put in can influence our results.

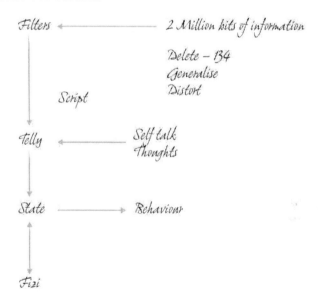

Your Doorman

Have you ever bought a new car, not necessarily brand new, but new for you? Did you notice how many other people were driving the same make and model? They weren't there before — or were they?

Or, if you and your partner are expecting a baby, suddenly there are people pushing prams all over the high street. It must be a baby boom! Or could it be that they were always there, but you did not notice them?

According to Mihaly Csikszentmihalyi, a Hungarian-born expert on the concept of *Flow*, a highly-focused mental state, we are bombarded with 2 million bits of information a second but the filters in our brain only allow 134 bits through.

So, your brain acts like a personal assistant, filtering out what it thinks is unusable data and allowing through that which is useful to us. This is all very well and stops you from becoming blitzed with a sensory overload, but its current settings might be filtering out some good stuff too! Our filters are made up of several things, including our beliefs, values, attitudes, memories and our language. Like the nightclub doorman, who only lets in people on management's list, your internal doorman only allows in information about the stuff that you are interested in or which you are already aware of.

This is useful in two ways; firstly, when we set goals our doorman will accept through information which is around us, but which is out of our conscious awareness, however, if it is relevant to our goals we will become conscious of it. It operates in the same way that you notice the cars which are the same make as your own.

If we have an opinion or make a judgement about someone, then information supporting that opinion or judgement will be what filters through. For example, if you think a colleague is negative then that is what you will notice about them. In order to make sense of the world we generalise, which means that one or two behaviours someone displays can cause us to make a judgment about that person. If a manager behaves in a directive manner and lacks emotional intelligence we may call them a poor manager.

The Doorman analogy allows your brain to filter through all the data so that you can make decisions quickly for survival and protection. It works by a combination of deleting, generalising and distorting information.

TIP—Practice using your doorman; observe all the good things that are happening in your team at work. Make a note of only the good things you see happening. When you do this, you will notice an immediate positive change in the way you regard the people around you.

Let's explore these concepts in more detail, building your knowledge and demonstrating how you can utilise it in your life.

Deletion

Every second, we receive around 2 million bits of information but only consciously process around 134 bits, this is so we don't get a sensory overload. But some of this deleted information could be very useful to us. This simple example illustrates my point:

Try counting the number of Fs in the following sentence…

FINISHED FILES ARE THE RESULT OF YEARS OF SCIENTIFIC STUDY COMBINED WITH THE EXPERIENCE OF YEARS OF WORK.

If you have not seen this brain teaser before, you probably said three. If you have seen it before you may have said six, but there are seven in this version. In the English language we pronounce the word 'of' with a 'V' sound, and, therefore, we don't tend to process the word 'of' as including the letter 'F'.

Without looking at your watch, I would like you to draw its face on a piece of paper. If you are not wearing a watch, draw a clock face which you are familiar with. Now compare your drawing to your watch, do you see any differences?

Some people draw numbers, but their watch has Roman numerals, or only has four numbers, most commonly twelve, three, six and nine. So, if you did not draw your watch correctly, why was that? The answer is quite simple, when you glance at your watch you are only interested in the time, the detailed design is less important, so it is filtered out. Even though you look at your watch many times a day, you can't remember exactly what it's like.

Already, you will have deliberately noticed people doing good stuff at work by focusing on the positive. Have you noticed your attitude towards people and teams changing for the better?

Generalisation

When you were first learning to talk, you probably pointed to a chair and your parents told you it was a chair. Then, perhaps, you would have pointed at a table and said "chair". You would have been corrected and taught the right word, and so you learnt about different types of furniture. That way, when you saw a different chair, you knew it was a type of chair. And, as an adult, when you meet someone who says they analyse tissue and fluid samples, you probably haven't got a clue what they are on about, but you do know they are a type of laboratory worker or scientist.

Generalisation is useful to build rapport and to understand the world around us. However, it is important to remember that we generalise and can form opinions about people and teams, or customers and suppliers, based on just one or two behaviours or events. A good leader will invest in building relationships across teams and departments and will be aware that what they see in a person is not everything there is to see.

For protection we have an in-built tribal instinct to stick with our own pack, superstitious of those from other tribes such as the sales department!

We notice when they do things that don't quite fit with our view of the way procedures should be followed. We form opinions and make judgements, then delete all the good stuff they do, such as bringing in new business, and only focus on the one or two behaviours we don't approve of. This judgement is an example of generalising and it can be damaging to the effective running of an organisation.

So, what can you do as a leader to improve relationships between teams? My advice would be to recognise the good work of others and focus your team's attention on the good things other departments are doing, in the same way I asked you to do with your own team. Being mean-spirited and judgemental are behaviours that are alien to top leaders, we no longer need the instincts that protected us 40,000 years ago. The finance department are not going to raid your office wielding calculators!

Distortion

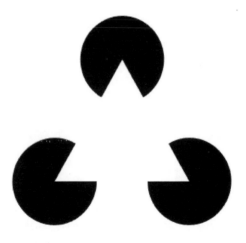

In the picture above can you see a white triangle? Actually, there isn't a white triangle there, but your brain distorts the image to make it fit with what it thinks it is or expects to be there.

Here's a simple example of what can happen in an everyday situation. Have you ever arrived at work a few minutes late and noticed your manager look up? Perhaps you thought, she's noticed that I'm late. But maybe she got distracted and was deep in thought. Your script, or model of reality, is telling you it is bad to be late, so it tricks you into reading the situation in a way that fits with your belief.

Everything that has come through your filters is stored and contributes to your model of reality or, as Richard Wilkins, the UK Minister of Inspiration calls it, your script. Your script is formed in your early years by your parents. Your 'script-writer' had his or her script written by someone who was probably born a long time ago. So, if your mum was born in the 1960s or 70s, her mum would probably have been born around the time of the Second World War. If your grandmother grew up in the UK, it would have been during times of depression, war, scarcity and rationing, so values such as not wasting food and eating all of your dinner may have been passed on to your mum as she was growing up. The belief in scarcity could have led to a need for security. There will have been all sorts of beliefs and values passed down through generations with the very best of intentions. If you listen to your Gran, you may hear her saying things like "don't get above your station", "money is the root of all evil", "good things come to those who wait" and "you are lucky to be in a good job".

Meanwhile, your mum may have encouraged you to get a good education and join a "blue chip" company. Our script makes us who we are, it is our blueprint for the way we experience the world and the events around us. It contains our deepest values and beliefs and creates our perceptions.

15

Essentially, we read from our script or, to use an NLP term, our model of the world, and compare anything we perceive to it. So, information is distorted to make sense with our script. Other people do the same thing, which can lead to misunderstandings and disagreements.

Zig Ziglar, suggested that many of us have a narrow view of who we are and how we see ourselves. He described himself as an optician who could fit you with a new pair of glasses so that you would see yourself in a new light. Zig also suggested that we don't necessarily need rose-tinted glasses to see the world around us, but we should definitely not be wearing "woes-tinted" glasses. Taking the theme further, Jamie Smart suggests that, at certain times, we see a situation with the wrong pair of glasses. I'd like to build on that concept a little.

Imagine if you had several pairs of glasses with which you could view the world from different perspectives: your sunglasses would make everything a little darker, the rose-tinted ones would offer a more optimistic view of life. You could even have a set of Coronation Street glasses that would make your life look like a soap opera, where there are several crises going on each week and life becomes a bit of a drama, it gets upsetting and makes you feel stressed and anxious.

How you perceive the reality of what is happening depends on which set of glasses you are wearing at that moment. They distort events and often magnify threats, making you feel bad. I'll let you into a secret. I expect you already know this intellectually, but you won't really get it until you start applying it. How you feel comes from your physiology and your thoughts, or your self-talk. Your feelings do *not* come from the world around you, they can only come from your thoughts. If you are feeling lousy or worried about something, you probably have your "Corrie" glasses on. You can change your glasses by acknowledging that your feelings are coming from your thoughts and the way you are thinking about something. Your script will trick you into thinking that something outside of you is making you feel this way. I'll keep coming back to this concept until you can apply it habitually.

I rather like the acronym for false evidence appearing real: FEAR. This occurs when our mind distorts information based on our belief system or script and we perceive it to be negative, that is when we can start worrying.

TIP — Are you worrying about something that has not occurred yet or only seeing the negative, whilst ignoring all the good things that are happening? Notice your take on information.

So, we have explored our filters and how they delete, generalise and distort information, next we will examine what happens to that information.

Like a television that can be altered in colour, contrast, brightness and sound, we too have an internal sensory system, or 'internal telly' that displays pictures, sounds, tastes, smells and touch. Earlier, I suggested that words on a page trigger images and they, in turn, trigger feelings. In NLP terminology, this is your internal representation.

We agreed that when you are feeling good and positive, you tend to approach the day differently and generally get some good results. Let's think about some useful ways that you can improve your state.

When you watch sport on the television they always have a commentator — and so do you — your internal

17

dialogue, or self-talk. Everyone talks to themselves (it is just known as thinking). Now, that voice inside your head is *your* voice, right? What I am going to do is show you how you can make that internal dialogue a lot more positive, so that it works for you.

There are unconscious thoughts that influence the internal representations in our internal telly and, therefore, affect our state. Then there are the thoughts we are conscious of, which have the same impact. And there are the words we use consciously when we talk to ourselves, these words can be either negative or positive, it's your choice! But whichever you choose will have an impact on your state and, therefore, on your behaviour and actions.

So, we can worry and paint negative pictures on our telly, and experience a negative state and possibly a negative outcome, or alternatively we can talk to ourselves positively and we will feel much happier and more confident about the situation. Be warned, it takes practice!

Your Inner Architect — The Way You Talk to Yourself

Muhammad Ali's declaration of "I am the greatest!" worked well for him. His ability to predict which round his opponent would go down in was legendary — "Archie Moore, you'll be down in four!"

His self-talk was spoken out loud to spook his opponents and to delight the spectators. But he worked hard in the gym and on the road to prepare physically. His mental preparation went hand in hand with the miles he covered. The preparation was what made him successful, not just dancing under the lights.

Okay, I don't expect you to go into a meeting with your colleagues and say out loud, "I'm a winner, that new

18

contract is mine for the taking!" But I do want you to be aware of what you are thinking and saying to yourself.

Positive self-talk takes practice. It changes your internal representation and your focus. It also paints pictures of the outcome you want.

An architect creates plans and uses models of the building they are creating, but it starts with their imagination. Your self-talk creates small goals and allows you to develop pictures of the steps towards the results you want.

Good examples of positive self-talk are:
I can do this!
I expect a good result.
This is going to be a great day!
I'm really up for it.
I'm going to play really well today.

TIP—Start using positive self-talk and be aware of your thoughts, if they are negative turn them into a positive.

A few years ago, I recognised that we could do something with our conscious thoughts, i.e. if we were aware of them we could consciously change our thoughts to be more positive, but I had not realised that we could do something about our more unconscious thoughts. That's until I came across Sydney Banks, a philosopher whose teachings started around the same time as the birth of NLP. Syd advocates that *"our feelings are a barometer for our thoughts"*. So, if we are feeling low or unhappy it must be a thought we are having and we can become more consciously aware of it. Then we can reflect on what is happening that may be causing us to distort events and information. He also says, "It's just a thought". So, with any negative emotion we are feeling we can say to ourselves "it's just a thought", and then work to change it. Remember, when we are feeling negative we are probably wearing our 'Corrie' glasses. It is not external events, which are making us feel bad, it is how we are *thinking* about those events. Take the 'Corrie' glasses off!

Several years ago, a business coach showed me an old YouTube video of a Bob Newhart sketch called *Stop It*. In the sketch he plays a therapist who is working with a woman who is very troubled. It begins like this:

"Hi, I'm Catherine."

"Bob," the therapist replies, "Tell me what the problem is Catherine?"

"I'm afraid I'll be buried alive in a box! Whenever I think about it I feel afraid."

The therapist asks, "Has anyone ever tried to bury you alive in a box?"

"No, but every time I think about it I feel truly awful!" she responds.

I'll leave it with you to watch the rest of the sketch. Enjoy!

My friend Mark, who is also into Sydney Banks, was running on a treadmill with his trainer egging him on to run a mile as fast as he possibly could. Mark was beginning to feel some pain and then he said to himself: "it's just a thought", and went on to do his fastest mile ever!

Using Syd's barometer analogy, awareness of how we are feeling can provide a feedback loop so that we can change the focus of our thoughts.

Negative self-talk concentrates our mind on what we don't want, which is not very helpful. For example, worrying about an upcoming exam is like negative goal setting, painting a picture in our mind's eye of what we don't want. Worrying to the point of being mildly anxious or fearful is not useful. In fact, it dramatically reduces our resources.

The emotion of fear has a positive intent, to protect us. I think the first sign of worry is a signal to act. I believe it is rather like a hazard warning. If you see some water spilt on a hospital ward or factory floor you would mop it up. It was very useful for our ancestors, to protect them from bad weather or other tribes, but maybe today sometimes it kicks in inappropriately.

A delegate once told me, "I'm worried about my leadership assignment."

"Have you started it yet?" I asked.

"No," he replied.

Often, when we take action the worry stops. There is a great line on a plaque in a churchyard in Cornwall: *Worry is like paying interest on problems that have not occurred yet!*

So, rather than worry, I would like you to ask yourself a better question. Once you start asking yourself better questions, your state changes and you are likely to have more forward momentum.

Here are some positive questions:

What result do I want?

How can I improve the situation?

Who can help me?

What haven't I done yet?

I find that asking myself better questions makes me more resourceful and is quicker and often more effective than positive self-talk. Of course, you can combine them. Paul McKenna states that, "questions determine the focus of our perception," and Sydney Banks suggests that our thoughts are like the rudder of a ship that steers us safely to open water or, alternatively, can lead us onto the dangerous rocks near the shore.

TIP—From now on, ask yourself better questions and reflect on your thoughts, remember, your feelings are a feedback loop to your thoughts and "it is just a thought". You will become more positive in your outlook and take charge of situations.

So, we delete, generalise and distort the information coming in and we get an internal representation. But it is not real, just our *representation* of the event, or our *take* on it. This impacts on our feelings, physiology and behaviour, which affects our results. We can change our internal representation with our self-talk, or by asking ourselves better questions and changing our glasses.

Chapter Three — Putting the Right Stuff In

Albert Einstein is often quoted as saying that insanity is "doing the same thing over and over again and expecting different results."

Some people wait for good things to happen without doing the good stuff we have been discussing. They complain about other people, they moan about their job, but still expect a good life. That used to be called GI GO, garbage in, garbage out, by computer programmers.

In the 1950s, Earl Nightingale made a recording entitled *The Strangest Secret.* He suggested the key to success was what you put into your mind. He argued that the human mind is like land, what you put into it will grow. So, if a farmer plants seeds of corn in the land then, sure enough, corn will grow. Likewise, if the farmer were to plant weeds, they would grow too. The land does not mind what crop is planted. Your garden, in the summer after a good dose of sunshine and rain, will have weeds popping up alongside your favourite plants. Before long, they smother them, making your lovely garden overgrown and untidy, in the same way that negative thoughts can smother your outlook.

Your mind is like fertile land and can be fed by your thoughts and the better questions you can start asking yourself. So, simple, eh? All you have to do is remember to talk to yourself in a positive way, put the right ingredients into the cake, feed the positive, blah, blah, blah. So, there you have it, the miracle cure, what you feed into your mind will impact on your state of mind and, therefore, on your results. Or will it?

Don't Look at the Vomit Applied to Leadership

Sorry to spoil your morning coffee and chocolate digestive, but I had to share a profound realisation I had while walking our cocker spaniel on Sunday morning. Ashby, where I live, is quite a respectable town, but at the top of the path leading from our road was the vilest pool of stuff. It drew my eyes, and, for a few moments, I let it spoil my walk.

On the way back, I deliberately gazed at a bush where a robin was perched. Interestingly, all I took in was the blue sky, and the bushes with the remaining red berries, and the robin. It was as if the you know what did not exist. In my perception, or reality, it was not there.

There were two distinct points I got from this:

1. Don't focus on the vomit or bad stuff. See all the good things that are happening. For example, your business results might be low after Christmas, but there are lots of new opportunities beginning to show. Your health and safety measures may be high in some areas, but you have senior managers signing up for the IOSH training. Or this month's sales are below budget, but new enquiries are high.

2. The second point, which is even more profound, was this: when I was not looking at the vomit it was not in my reality or perception because I was looking the other way. What if the vomit was something good, which I'm not seeing because in my perception and filters I can't see it? In other words, in my world it does not exist. A simple example of this could be a person who operates a machine in your work place, or perhaps picks stock, or someone who works in customer service, helping with enquiries. Imagine if they had not been given the opportunities or encouragement you or I have had. They are in a job, and that is pretty much their lot in life (or so they believe), they would not dream of applying for the shift team leader position possibly due to fear of rejection.

The same could apply to a manager that reports to you, who has never expressed a wish to go any further but is possibility limiting themselves by what they can't see.

However, by building relationships with the people you work with, they will open up to you and that is when you can help them see new possibilities.

You probably don't realise this, but your ancestors were probably a bunch of negative b******ds. You have evolved from tribes who were conditioned to focus on danger and threats. We have what is known as a negativity bias, which means that we focus more on the negative than the positive. This was essential for survival, the hard-wiring in the amygdala part of our brain would amplify threats over other events. This cave person thinking still kicks in today, causing the production of cortisol which floods through our system to give us the energy to fight or flight. But when the stock market drops 20 points we don't need to run fast or start a fight, so we become stressed. Our brain waves go from an alpha state to a beta frequency, and too much beta activity causes anxiety, stress and a lack of perspective.

The fall in the stock market would also be analysed by the so-called experts on *Newsnight*. Their opinions would then be revisited and re-analysed by another set of experts the next morning on the breakfast radio news and, hey presto, we could be talking about another recession.

Not only do *we* have a tendency to focus on the vomit, but many people around us do too. This makes it very difficult to maintain perspective and keep up with the positive self-talk and saying to yourself "it is just a thought". In fact, just staying ahead of the gloom mongers when you believe your economic well-being is about to crash onto the rocks is exhausting.

There are numerous examples of this type of threat. In the late 1990s, the big scare was the Millennium bug, when it was predicted that the world's IT systems would crash. Many companies paid their IT staff a bonus to hang on to them. Tony Blair stated it was "one of the most serious problems facing, not only British business, but the global economy today." (*BBC News*, 31st December 2014.) Mr. Blair also told us that Iraq had weapons of mass destruction so maybe we should have seen that one coming. So, what actually happened as the new century dawned? Apparently, a bus driver in Australia was unable to collect a fair with his machine, but apart from that... well nothing.

Next, we had bird flu, then swine flu, then we were told the economy would collapse if we voted to leave the EU.

But, never fear, help is here with your new sparkly set of super-vision spectacles. I'm going to suggest some steps you can take to set you back on track, it might be that you use all these steps or just those that work best for you.

Firstly, you have to remember that you are wearing your 'Corrie' glasses and that you have a negativity bias, so any event will be amplified.

Next, say to yourself, "I'm wearing my Corrie glasses and my feelings about this, i.e. my anxiety, is not coming from the event, but my thoughts."

Syd Banks suggested that, in the same way our body heals itself after a wound, our mind could too, given a little time. Allow your mind to relax back into the slower alpha state of calm. You can do this by meditating or going for a walk. Put on your super-vision glasses and look down on the event from a point in space. I like to imagine that I'm observing an event on earth from the moon. It makes the event seem fairly insignificant.

The final step is to immerse your feelings in all the good things you have in life and dwell within those feelings for several minutes. According to Dr. Rick Hanson, this will allow new neuron pathways to build to combat the lower-level, cave person, limbic reaction.

In my earlier training days, I would dwell on the feedback I had received on the evaluation forms. If eleven people had scored 8, 9 or 10 out of 10 and one had scored a five, I would focus on the lower score during my journey home. It was only years later that I learned that the delegates were actually scoring themselves! Remember what the big boy Einstein said.

NLP is about putting the right ingredients into your mind and taking action. It is about focusing on the results you want, and not those you don't. It is about being aware of the information around you, good and bad, but not over emphasising the bad stuff.

TIP — Monitor your feelings, notice when you are wearing your 'Corrie' glasses and realise that when you are feeling negative it is because you are looking through the wrong spectacles. Remember, your feelings come from your thoughts, not what is happening in Coronation Street, or worse, EastEnders!

Chapter Four—The Language You Use with Other People

Let me tell you a secret that you are not taught at school. Your words are magical! Let me explain how.

Your language is very powerful, it can paint pictures, it can affect moods, it can motivate. We have a whole section on language coming up later, but I want to introduce you to some hints and tips you can start with straight away.

Have you thought about the impact your words have on other people? Some years ago, a delegate on a senior leadership programme recounted a conversation with her husband. She told us that learning about some basic NLP had made her speak differently to her husband. She informed us that he was out of work and attending interviews. Prior to our course, she explained she would ask him if he was nervous before an interview and he would reply that he was. That morning though, she asked him if he was feeling positive and he responded that he was. To our great delight, we learned that he was offered the job!

So, every time you speak with someone it changes his or her internal telly! I used to ask my son, Josh, "What's the best thing you did at school today?"

"Coming home," he would reply.

No, seriously, he'd tell me about football at break or PE, or something funny that had happened with one of his mates.

We can also reframe situations for people by asking them a question or letting them see a different context. For example:

"Oh, it's raining again!"

"Yes, but it's helping your garden."

OR

"I've had a meeting cancelled with an important customer!"

"That will give you time to think about your marketing strategy. You've been telling me for weeks you haven't had time to do it and now you have!"

When we are coaching, we ask the coachee better questions, such as, "What would good look like?", which creates internal representations for them.

Our words and language shape our reality and the meaning we give to situations and events. For every word we speak we get an internal representation, and so does the person we are talking too. Let me give you an example of how words influence our state. Say to yourself out loud "I failed". Now say, "That's not the result I wanted". Which feels better?

Of course, Rogers and Hammerstein knew about this stuff years ago, with the *My Favourite Things* song from *The Sound of Music*. "*Raindrops on roses and whiskers on kittens, bright copper kettles and warm woollen mittens.*" In the film, Marie sang this to the children to take their minds off the storm.

Here's the thing. Negatives can be really useful. First of all, try this, don't think about a blue tree. What are you thinking about? A blue tree. We have to get an internal representation of what we don't want first. Let's try another. Don't think about someone you like! You can't help it, can you?

Once, on a training course, a waitress served our sandwiches and fruit in the hotel dining room where other people were eating a Sunday lunch, and then said to our delegates, "Ignore the smell of the Sunday roast". Of course, that's what they all noticed. It's also useful for golf too: "Watch out for the rough" or "ignore the water". But how many people use negatives in their language when asking children to something? "Don't talk", "Don't play on the road" and "Don't be late". All the kids do is get the internal representation of what you don't want them to do… "Don't spill that drink on the new carpet!"

TIP—Say what you want the outcome to be. Make sure your words create positive internal representations for people. For example, if you have a problem at work ask your team, "How would you like it to look?"

How We Use Metaphors

Jesus was with a bunch of his mates, about twelve in all, and they were just not getting it. He wanted them to spread his word (when he had gone), and recruit people to his teachings. The leader, Peter, was a simple fisherman and he was a tough nut to crack. So, Jesus tried this on them. "Go and be fishers of men."

"Ah," they replied.

We use metaphors to describe our grasp on an external event, but it is based on our internal reality (script) and belief, which then colours the event itself.

If you can change someone's metaphor you can significantly change their view of the world and their take on situations. A senior manager once told me that the integration of their business with another large corporation was going to be "a car crash".

I replied, "Could you see it like a first date?"

She smiled and then laughed.

Before I set up as a consultant, a colleague in the company I worked for said consultancy was either "feast or famine". Meaning that, if you do well then expect no work a few months later. I chose to ignore his remark, because he had no personal experience of being a self-employed consultant, but my negativity bias could have kicked in.

Metaphors in business are very common. I did a workshop earlier this year and the company accountant was telling everyone that "business is a battle", "if you can't beat them, join them", "it's dog eat dog out there". It occurred to me that his thinking and belief about the environment his company was operating in was hardly positive and would probably impact on his decision-making. So, his metaphors were defining the way he saw the world.

TIP—I would like you to notice the metaphors that you are using and, if they are negative, think of an alternative.

Some metaphors we hear at work include: climb the ladder, get to the top, take the long view, time is money, (it's not, by the way!). Or be ahead of the game, dead wood, regrouping, going into battle. Often, in a management meeting, they are used in abundance. People use metaphors to describe what they believe about something, which can help you assess your colleagues', coachees' and team's thinking. Remember, if you can change their metaphor, it will influence their thinking about a situation. Donald Trump told his followers that it was time to "drain the swamp", whatever he meant by that it didn't sound very productive or positive.

Because our language is a filter, not only will we filter out words we don't understand, especially Mandarin in my case, but our language also labels and gives meaning to events. So, the example of a business merger being like a car crash gave a different meaning to the event than if it was described as a first date. And when you change the meaning of something you will allow information through your filters that you would not have done previously.

Our language and metaphors are a clue to what is going on in our script or belief system, so a negative metaphor used by someone you are conversing with can indicate their perception about the topic you are discussing.

Chapter Five — Let it Shine!

Here is a fact: happy, positive people make better work colleagues; people will enjoy their company more. Happier people tend to focus less on problems and ask themselves better questions. They have less time for negative emotions and thoughts. They make decisions quicker. According to Martin Seligman and Kim Cameron, they generally have fewer health problems and live longer.

People will want to be around you if you are cheerful and positive. However, if you are surrounded by negativity it is much harder to maintain your attitude. The people you mix with have an impact on you. Spending time with people who are happy and positive will rub off on you and if that means joining a club and mixing with other positive people outside of work then do it! The most successful leaders I've observed don't put others down or criticise, and they don't waste time moaning and complaining. I think when people have a BMW about another person (think about it, W stands for whine), it is their negativity bias kicking in, plus the generalising filters only allowing one or two behaviours to get through. It helps people with low self-esteem feel better about themselves, but only has a short-term benefit. In fact, it will make them even more negative and less attractive to be with. But because we know about negativity bias we can show them a little compassion, they are just wearing their 'Corrie' glasses.

As a leader you can give yourself a positive 'feel good' at any time. Performing an act of kindness or doing something good for someone else produces the chemical oxytocin, which makes us happy. There is an old film called *Pay It Forward*, with the young Haley Joel Osment, in which, as part of a school project, our lead character invents a process where he does a favour for three different people without expecting anything in return, except that *they* have to do something good for three other people and so on.

Martin Seligman and Sydney Banks both believe that happiness is the foundation for producing good results and I believe it is the same as inside-out thinking. Our script tells us we will be happy when something good outside of us occurs.

Feeling positive about what you have already achieved is the starting point for appreciative inquiry, which is a process of asking questions to achieve the result you want and is the opposite of traditional problem solving. Here is an example:

Scenario — We are losing lots of customers' baggage at the arrivals terminal. ('Corrie' glasses firmly in place!)

Traditional Approach — Define the problem, measure it, (blame other departments), implement solutions, monitor and control.

Appreciative Inquiry Approach — Ask the team to share examples of where they have given excellent customer service in any context or situation, this will set them up into a positive resourceful state. Then ask them to imagine that they had awoken from a long deep sleep and come into work to find that all customers were receiving an excellent arrivals experience. Then get them to draw pictures of what was happening on a flip chart. Finally (and keep it past tense) ask them what they did to get there. They can then present this back.

Appreciative inquiry questions work well with coaching.
"Tell me what it will be like when you have successfully implemented your project?"

"What will Jodie be able to achieve when you spend time delegating and coaching her?"

Wishing for Bad News

Last Saturday, at the end of the Ashes win in Birmingham. I thought I would try and get tickets for the final test in Nottingham for Josh and me. The very nice lady said, "We only have them for day five (Monday), but you get your money back if they finish on Saturday or Sunday."

So, I booked, though I wasn't very hopeful. But she said, rather cheerfully, "It might rain on Friday and Saturday." Anyway, I've spent all week hoping for rain. It rained yesterday when I came back from Liverpool and it rained today in Ashby.

I'm a big believer in starting with myself before teaching others, so I've worked hard at being positive over the last few years. It's not natural for me to wish for everyone's weekend to be spoilt with bad weather, especially those who have paid £85 a ticket for a seat behind the wicket. So, it has been rather unnatural for me to break the habit. That's right, if you are positive and cheerful for long enough, it becomes a habit.

I've just checked the forecast for the next five days and it's sunny every day. I do hope the BBC gets it wrong!

Here is an idea for an activity I picked up from Jamie Smart's book, *Clarity*. I often ask delegates at conferences "What makes you happy?" and they give me a long list including people smiling, family, sunny days and holidays. Then I ask, "Is it those things or *thinking about them* which makes you happy?"

When we were in a holiday apartment in Devon with a beautiful view of the beach and the sea I said to Josh, age eleven at the time, "Wow, what a view!"

37

To which he replied, "Yeah, right, has the apartment got a Wi-Fi connection?"

You see, I associated the view with happy thoughts and it was those thoughts that made me happy.

Let's take it from another angle, when I asked the same conference delegates "what makes you unhappy?" they responded with things like: people moaning, the news, the rain and paying parking fines. And, you guessed it, I asked, "is it those things or *thinking about them* which makes you unhappy? Or possibly the way you think about them?"

If we accept that our thoughts directly impact our feelings, then it is our thoughts which make us happy or unhappy. You are probably still only getting it intellectually, but I'll keep plugging away!

Chapter Six — Modelling Excellence

Brace yourself for a bit of history, I'll keep it fairly brief. John Grinder and Richard Bandler created NLP in the 1970s. Their goal was to discover why some therapists produced excellent results using the English language. They based their work on people such as Virginia Satir and Milton Erikson who achieved excellent outcomes with their clients by the way they talked to them and the language they listened for and utilised themselves. Then Richard and John created models to allow other people to assimilate the same processes. Over the years, many people were modelled in different fields and a host of techniques were developed as other contributors joined in. So, NLP is about modelling excellence which has led to a large number of 'apps' or techniques for communication, rapport, goal setting, getting rid of fears, phobias and negative emotions, internal conflict and blockages in our thinking, or what we call 'limiting beliefs', which may hold us back.

NLP, at its most basic, is about re-programming your brain, or other people's brains, so that you/they operate more effectively.

We can take the concept of modelling into our everyday lives in its simplest form. Master practitioners of NLP, will use a process whereby they take someone who is an expert in something and elicit their values, i.e. the unconscious and conscious things that are important to them. This will tell them what their subject's motivation is for doing whatever it is they are doing.

They then ask them what they believe about what they are doing. For example, if you were to model me when I demonstrate a technique during NLP practitioner training, you would ask, "What do you believe about this?"

And I would respond that it was going to be a total success if the delegate does what I ask them to.

After discovering the values and the beliefs the expert has about what they are doing the master practitioner of NLP would then elicit the strategy or unconscious steps the expert takes throughout the process.

They may ask, "what is the first thing that happens? Is it something you see, or something you hear, or something you say to yourself or a feeling you get?"

And they might say, "I say something to myself, I say, its time! And then I get a feeling of conviction."

"Where is the feeling?"

They might respond, "it's in my shoulders."

"Okay, what happens next?" Then they keep repeating this until we have all the steps in their process to success.

Then the master practitioner would watch them do it and observe their physiology, how they stand, the steps they take, and would ask lots of questions to understand why and what they are doing.

The subject is probably not conscious of this process, because it has become an unconscious routine.

You can take the concept and apply it in a lighter fashion. Let us suppose you are working hard, but not getting the result you want. By modelling you can discover what others are already doing to achieve similar results to those you want. If you talk with someone in your own organisation, or outside, who is getting better results than you it is likely that you can replicate their actions and the level of effort they are putting in.

TIP—Find people who are getting a good result in your chosen field or in a field in another sector that parallels where you want to improve. Ask them questions about what they believe about what they are doing. For example, an expert in telemarketing has a total belief in her client's products and services. So, she is in the right mind-set when making a call. Then follow the steps they take until you can do the process yourself.

A Warning about NLP

There is a lot about NLP on the web and quite a few people trained in the subject, however, many use the jargon that was created by some of the original contributors who possibly wanted to make it appear scientific. Be warned if you start using the terminology you've found on the internet like presuppositions, complex equivalence, epistemology and synaesthesia, yawn, yawn, yawn...

It will lose the very people you want to build rapport with. Much better to keep things simple and be *you*, but a better you!

Whatever you want to be good at requires much more than technical knowledge. In fact, it probably involves developing a core know-how using a combination of two or three skills or behaviours that together are in demand and provide a competitive edge.

For example, a great leadership trainer may have read widely on the subject and had management experience, but also has learned to simplify the content and put it across in a funny, engaging way using everyday examples and stories people can relate to, and that's the part that differentiates. Likewise, if you, the leader or coach, is happy, positive and continually educating yourself, you will have an advantage, providing you adopt the new habits you are reading about. But, here is the thing; people don't get on board with complicated stuff, so keep your message and communication simple. We recommend certain books to delegates on our leadership programmes, some are there to inform and others to use for referencing for the more advanced qualifications. Often the terminology overcomplicates a simple meaning. For example, one book uses the terms: "idealized influence", which means 'walk the talk' and display the values you want others to adopt, and "individualized consideration" means coach your team. Why don't they just say that?

Simplicity

Last night I attended a maths class at Joshua's primary school. There I was, sat on a plastic red chair, in a year six classroom, barely able to get my knees under the table. Only three days before I had been invited to teach some head teachers about NLP and here I was 'tables-turned' (a metaphor).

The teacher was great; he started off telling us the reason why the school was changing the maths' curriculum. Let me tell you, the secretary of state for education is regarded by some teachers as a bit of a 'toff villain' who wants kids to learn by rote, like he did in the early seventies at his public school.

But here was Mr C explaining that the government had researched education in other countries to look at how they achieve excellent results and also at exam results in the UK. He explained that research demonstrated that children doing exams at sixteen years of age who got grade D, were often just as intelligent as kids who got grade C. But they were slower in answering the questions!

This is where we got back to basics! If children could use faster methods, they would get more marks! So, an end to 'super chunking' and back to 'long division'.

"Yeah!" said the mums and dads.

Mr C also said if a child can recite their times tables then it helps with most maths! Apparently, in tables there are 78 to remember, e.g., 4 x 5 =20. But, he informed us, if you take out the ones, twos and tens, there are only 45 to learn and if you remember every nine adds up to a nine that's only 36 to learn! Oh, and wait, if you take out the fives because they are half of 10, that's 29 having taken out the 10 x 5!

Let's start by making things simple. If your job is an IT manager, then don't call yourself head of information system solutions, Europe and South-East Asia. You can't fit it on a business card for one thing and everyone else still calls you the IT department!

And, finally, if you keep things simple you remember your purpose, why you became a nurse or a police officer in the first place and it's important that you keep reminding your team of that every day, particularly when they are facing cost cuts and change!

Mr C is a brilliant teacher because, he tells the kids why they are learning something, he gives them simple methodologies, he makes it fun and he gives praise. You can do those four simple things with your team, can't you?

Leadership is truly simple then, it is about being inspired yourself and having a purpose. And then, through delegating and coaching, encouraging others to discover that flame inside them or switch on their lights!

Chapter Seven—Your Missed Opportunities: Sliding Doors

Let me start this chapter off by saying that everything in your head is not necessarily real. Sure, events outside of you may occur, but it is your interpretation of those events that make your reality. Essentially, you are living in a world inside your own head, your own filters, governed by your script and negativity bias, will select what you allow through. This will then be interpreted by you and become your reality. Once we recognise that our reality does not come from *outside* of us but from *inside*, we can change our reality or what is going on around us by changing our thinking. Our thinking then determines what actions we *decide* to take, and our actions will lead to new opportunities and growth.

Let me give you a simple example. One of our delegates decided to speak with her teenage daughter in an adult to adult manner. The outcome of which was to fundamentally change her daughter's usual response and the conversation moved on to spending a weekend away together. This had a significant impact on her reality.

Do you remember the film *Sliding Doors* where the hero was unfairly dismissed from her job, a little girl stepped in front of her as she ran down the steps to the platform and missed her train? She was then mugged and arrived home later that day to greet her boyfriend coming out of the shower. She could not get a job and ended up delivering sandwiches by day and waiting tables by night to support her failing writer of a boyfriend.

However, her other self made it onto the train, got home and caught her boyfriend with another woman. She stormed out of the apartment and went to stay with her friend; she had a new haircut so we could distinguish between her two selves. Then she started a new marketing business and met the man she deserved.

We all have 'sliding door' moments. For example, I could have leased my waterfront flat in Leeds, but second mortgages were rare at the time and maybe I did not allow myself the opportunity to discover what was available. So, I sold it at a slight loss, whereas now it would have been paid off and I'd have a decent amount of capital.

So, how do we recognise these 'sliding door' moments? Some are off our radar, particularly if we have beliefs that limit us. In other words, we don't even notice an opportunity. Others, we are more consciously aware of but may not grasp because they don't fit with our values, which is fair enough. You may offer me the role of a getaway driver, but it is not for me, thanks. On the other hand, some opportunities we might consider pursuing but talk ourselves out them because of an unconscious lack of self-belief.

'Sliding door' moments occur on a daily basis, such as questioning whether to go to the pub or not, but perhaps some of those with a greater magnitude occur less frequently. Such examples might include; noticing a job posting but not applying for it because you may believe you are under-qualified, or, when talking with a friend who has set up their own business, you consider what it would be like to do something similar yourself, then dismiss the idea as not doable.

I'd like you to start being really consciously aware of these 'sliding door' moments in your life, write them down on your notes page. Ask yourself the following questions:

1. *Do I want this? If the answer is no, ask why not?*

2. Is the answer of no possibly because of a limiting belief?
   3. If it is, ask yourself who is the most successful or effective person I know and what would they do in this situation?

What I'm saying is that you can influence your world from the inside by thinking and behaving differently. You have probably done this many times before, like when you decided not to give up on a goal or when you plucked up the courage to talk with someone you did not know and got yourself a date! The concept of creating your own world is very liberating, but is alien to our script.

Let's examine the creation of a script or model of reality. Most of us go to school because that is what everyone does and it's free! We also get free health and dental care as we are processed through the sausage machine of formal education, learning stuff about Pythagoras, differentiation and adverbs. We learn to blame outside events on our setbacks, "the Wi-Fi is poor", "my mum did not get me up in time", "the English teacher is rubbish". We have to have the latest phone, fashion and hairstyle because the advertisers constantly tell us it will make us feel good. The endless mind control seeps out of the TV showing perfect people living perfect lives that we can have too, and we only have to subscribe for £22.50 a month. Then we get something called a job, in which we are given a grade and a pay level and learn to know our place in the hierarchy. We may save for a two-week holiday in the Canaries but feel rubbish on the last day because we are going back to work tomorrow.

And pretty soon we become conditioned with the belief that our happiness comes from good things occurring outside of us. The government herd us around like cattle knowing what is best for us. (I'm getting on my soapbox now!) Twenty years ago, they persuaded us to buy diesel because it reduced carbon emissions. Then we discovered its particles were causing premature deaths and breathing difficulty for many adults and children. Bus lanes were introduced into our cities causing traffic to clog up, using even more fuel, which made the situation worse. They encouraged more young people to go to university and get a degree, then they decided universities could charge our young people £30,000 for the privilege. Parents who were not sure about running up a huge debt felt pressurised by what society would think if their son or daughter did not go to university. Today, those same parents are worried about their diesel car being worth less than a Mars bar.

Limiting Beliefs

It was Christmas morning and our son Joshua came bounding onto the bed with a pillow case stuffed with presents from Santa, which was a bit much for a sixteen-year-old to be doing at 7.15am. Only kidding, he was five.

"Daddy, daddy, daddy!" he yelled as he bounced up and down on the bed holding an opened present in his hand. "It's PlayStation Cars, just like Harvey's got!" He didn't realise he had nothing to play it on as he exuded excitement. On going downstairs though, he got his PlayStation! As I opened the curtains, he saw the crumbs on the floor where Santa had wolfed down the mince pie, the chewed end of the carrot the reindeer had left and the dregs of sherry at the bottom of the glass. "Look daddy, he's been!"

So, we don't believe what we see, we see what we believe. Every 'sliding door' moment is an opportunity, but because

48

of self-limiting beliefs we either don't see it or dismiss it. What if we could change those beliefs that hold us back? With NLP, we can.

Sir John Whitmore in *Coaching for Performance* quotes Tim Gallwey from his book, *The Inner Game of Tennis,* in which he said, "The opponent on the other side of the net is less powerful than the one inside your head." This means your beliefs, together with your self-talk, have a massive impact on your game, whatever it is.

Many of us see ourselves in a pretty one-dimensional way, like Zig Ziglar's analogy about fitting new glasses, yet we are more than that. We have a tendency to label ourselves and that becomes our identity. Often, when you meet with someone they will ask you what you do for a living. But what you do is not the same as who you are! You have enormous potential; your career could change several times. Until now you have possibly limited yourself in some way, living without realising it consciously. Like an autopilot our unconscious mind has been programmed over the years to complete numerous tasks habitually, which means we can effortlessly tie a shoelace or drive a car without thinking about it. This has obvious advantages, but can mean that we become less creative and approach new opportunities or challenges with 'in groove' thinking. If you are familiar with the 'new' technology of vinyl records you will know that a stylus follows a groove in a record, which is pretty much how our thinking works.

So, what keeps us doing similar things, why don't we experiment? Our comfort zones play a big part in keeping us from changing. We are happy to sing in the car but would not sing in public. Our comfort zone will prevent us from leaving an organisation and taking on a new role because of fear of the unknown. Some of us go to the same holiday destinations, year after year! Our ancestors who emigrated called the new places after the old country, with names such as New York and Melbourne. They had their own clubs and taught the world how to play cricket. These days we go to Spain and eat fish and chips and drink in the Irish pub! We are regulated like a thermostat on a wall, only allowing the room to fluctuate between 19 and 21 degrees.

The following is an article my son wrote for our company blog:

An Article by Josh Kay, Year 8, Age 12

People see secondary school as something scary and intimidating. In some cases, this is true, but it is also an opportunity to progress and try new things.

When I started at Ivanhoe College I was very nervous, because I thought I wouldn't be able to cope with all the things that came my way and I wanted to stay at primary because I thought that that's where I would be most comfortable.

However, when I got to grips with the work and the way things worked at Ivanhoe, I realised that all the changes that had happened at the start of the year were all for the better and that I should not worry about it, because I now know that it will all make me a better person and will help me have a good future.

If I was to say anything to the year 7 students that are joining, I would just tell them to have a positive attitude, because school can only be as good as you make it.

And that was with no prompting from me! Do you remember the stories you were told before moving up to secondary school? It was enough to scare any eleven-year old. In today's world they have a trial for two days to get them used to it and assimilate the new schedule.

Your Automatic Pilot—'Brain Robot'

So, what maintains your comfort zone? It's your unconscious mind. Going back to the driving example, do you remember learning to drive? You had to operate the clutch and the accelerator at the same time and, if you were doing a hill start, lift the handbrake off as well! Impossible! Oh, and indicate, look in the mirror and over your shoulder, then you stalled. But, after a while, you got the hang of it and did not even notice what you were doing. Now you can do your make-up, change radio channels and make a call, all in the middle lane. The automatic pilot has taken over. You have gone into 'brain robot' mode.

Our brain robot enables us to do many things unconsciously. However, if you were on a boat and you set the automatic pilot to the east and then turned the wheel north the boat would correct itself and continue east. Our unconscious mind controls all our habits and keeps us consistent. If you live in the UK and take your car to France, apart from driving on the right-hand side of the road, which feels odd, you will come to a roundabout and have to think about which way to look. I remember Dawn, my wife, shouting, "Look left!"

After a while I got used to it. In fact, I wanted to enjoy our holiday, so I consciously decided to tough it out for two weeks. After a few days it felt normal as my brain robot reprogrammed itself.

So, if you want to do new things expect to feel uncomfortable. Picture in your mind what you want to do, imagine doing it and get uncomfortable. What actually happens is that when you put yourself outside of your comfort zone and gain new levels of competence you are creating new neuron pathways and developing your neurology.

Chapter Eight — Limiting Beliefs

Limiting Beliefs — James Bond Cars on Top Gear

I was looking forward to watching the rerun of Richard Hammond's Top Gear *special last night. The programme tracked the* Bond *cars from the first films. I still remember watching in awe as the Aston Martin DB5 from* Gold Finger *spewed black smoke over a pursuing baddie, only to learn that there was a small man in the boot with a smoke machine. And that the underwater submarine Lotus from* The Spy Who Loved Me *was not really in the sea, it was a model in a tank, and they used Alka Seltzer tablets to create the bubbles. No way! A shattered belief!*

I guessed that the Moonraker space station was a model, but not the ejector seat in the DB5 or the underwater Lotus destroying a helicopter. What else have I believed because my imagination was distorting the event?

Several hundred years ago, we believed that the earth was flat. Until Roger Banister broke the four-minute-mile it was seen as physically impossible, once he had done it though, others quickly followed. In 1999, Hicham El Guerrouj ran it in 3.43.13 minutes, a huge advance.

I've already told you about our family Santa story and we have suggested that you don't believe what you see, you see what you believe.

Let's call the beliefs, which limit us in some way, 'limiting beliefs'. The first and deepest limiting beliefs are often taken on under the age of seven.

Beliefs can appear to be very solid, like the top on a four-legged table. The table legs are like reference points in our lives, where we have taken on beliefs that we can't *do* or *be* something. Often these references are adopted unconsciously. In other words, we are not aware that we are taking on a limiting belief, events just happen. When we are five and our teacher comments on our painting of a house by saying, "what a lovely cat", we don't think "that's it, I don't believe in myself!"

It is very subtle and is only noticeable by our actions. But years later we'll use expressions such as "I can't paint." A belief can be taken on by a single event, but is made even more pronounced by subsequent events, which is why I used the table leg analogy.

Morris Massey, a sociologist, described three major periods where our values and beliefs form.

The Imprint Period is up to the age of 7. We take on values and beliefs from those around us, our parents, close family and school. Sometimes, limiting beliefs can come from our parents. A few years ago, when Josh was about six, he used to ask me questions like "which formula one team do you think I'll drive for before I join Ferrari?" You don't get more certain than that!

I remember Dawn asking me why I carried on letting him think he would do it.

"Why not?" I asked.

"Because when he grows up he'll be too tall," she replied.

It was only a few months later that I discovered that Mark Webber, who used to be with Red Bull Racing, was six foot tall! Anyway, Josh got his own limiting belief when he came off at a sharp bend, sailed four feet into the air and up a bank on his first go in a motorised petrol kart at the age of eight. Apparently, no one has done that before on that particular track, at least he set a record!

Next, there is the Modelling Period, between the ages of eight and fourteen. I wanted to be James Bond when I was nine, kids these days have other heroes, just make sure yours have the right one!

The Socialisation period is between the ages of 14 and 21. We like being with people of our own age in groups. A head teacher once told me that from 14 years to 17 years, the kids would group closely together, it was only after this age that they mixed more readily with adults.

Our beliefs and values, or script, combine with other attributes to develop our filters or doorman. We then delete, generalise and distort what is coming in. Hence, we see what we believe. So, if we can alter our belief about ourselves we will see opportunities that we have not noticed before and we will have the confidence to take hold of them. Remember, at the lowest level, it is unconscious.

We may be consciously aware that we can't do something, expressed as *I can't do maths* or *I can't be a director*. This might not be the way we express it. Someone might not believe that they can ever be a director, so they don't set it as a goal. You might hear them say, "I am happy doing what I'm doing". And, of course, they might be! Other limiting beliefs that we are consciously aware of might be: *I don't believe I can get a BMW* or *I can't paint*. These are surface beliefs that limit us.

Surface beliefs	x x x x x
Unconscious	xxxx
Lower	x

Often the lowest level limiting beliefs are so unconscious that most people are not aware of them. Usually they can be identified if the coachee has two or more surface level beliefs and you ask, "what's underneath that?"

There are some people who don't have any limiting beliefs or have worked out that "actually, nothing can hold me back". There are many though who are acting in accordance with their beliefs, but they are not aware of what they are. Remember to take this into account when you are coaching someone.

Another indicator of a limiting belief is when someone is using reasons, such as, "I can't do that because…"

It is useful when coaching to listen for reasons so that you can explore them with your coachee for limiting beliefs.

I would like you to take a little time to think about, and maybe even write down, all the reasons you are using in your life. I'll start you off:

I can't lose weight because I'm big boned.

The economy is not very good.

They won't let me do that.

When you are using reasons, you are wearing your Coronation Street glasses, your take on situations is coming from your script.

Limiting beliefs can also be recognised from statements which people make, such as *I'm not capable* or *I can't make that sort of money*.

Some limiting beliefs, such as *I can't decorate* or *I can't do DIY*, are okay to hang onto!

There are two ways of removing limiting beliefs. The first is an NLP technique called 'submodality limiting belief change,' which I will explain later. The second is to use Time Line Therapy®. It is a linguistic coaching tool, which reframes events from your past. It was created in the 1980s in America by Tad James, and trade-marked when 'therapy' was more commonly used. The term 'timeline' is widely known in America, in fact, Facebook use it and it has become more common terminology in Europe.

We create new beliefs when we achieve goals, so goal setting, delegating and coaching produce growth and new beliefs.

Chapter Nine — Taking Personal Responsibility

"You cannot change the circumstances, the seasons, or the wind, but you can change yourself. That is something you have charge of." — Jim Rohn

Have you ever wondered what happens to the litter strewn by the side of the motorway? More importantly, who drops it? Does the driver think to him or herself: "I know, I'll open the window and chuck my McDonald's bag out and it will disappear into thin air?"

These days, local government spends thousands of pounds hiring litter pickers to work in dangerous conditions so that drivers who won't take personal responsibility don't have to put their takeaway wrappers in a bin at their next stop.

Obviously, none of these drivers work for your organisation, or do they? If so, what are they like at work? Lack of personal responsibility usually manifests itself through blaming someone or something else, or leaving dirty coffee mugs in the sink. You may hear the following from such colleagues: *the information from engineering was not clear, they have reduced our budget... we can't do anything,* blah blah blah. As mentioned earlier, Syd Banks describes this as outside-in thinking, where you believe events outside of you are affecting your feelings or state, when actually it is only your thoughts which impact on how you feel about a situation.

Taking personal responsibility is key to business effectiveness, yet so few organisations train their managers and employees in this, dare I say it, *life changing* concept. Just sit back in your chair for a minute and imagine what your organisation would feel like if everyone took personal responsibility. Personal responsibility is the corner stone of both NLP and coaching and impacts massively on your results. We all *think* we take personal responsibility, it is only when we are consciously aware of our thoughts and our self-talk that we may become aware that we are not. Richard Bandler asked the question, "Who is driving your bus?"

When I ask delegates, "If your life was a bus, where are you sitting on it?" Many reply: "I'm driving it". Some say they are the conductor, which is strange because we haven't had conductors since 1970! Others say they would like to be driving the bus, but they know that they are not.

In some areas or schools of NLP they refer to personal responsibility as personal power. A little Californian for me! However, when you do take responsibility the impact on your results in life will be huge.

Zig Ziglar jokes that blaming someone else has been around since Adam and Eve. When God asked Adam if he had eaten fruit from the forbidden tree, Adam pointed at Eve and replied, "It was her. She gave it to me, honest!"

When God asked Eve if that was true, she blamed the snake!

Often, you will hear reasons, these are subtler than excuses. But, most of the time, neither the speaker or the listener are aware of an excuse being used. A few years ago, I was working with a corporate client, doing our *How to be a Better You* workshop. One of the delegates shared her experience with the group. She agreed with me that her physiology does indeed affect her state. "I go running for half a mile every morning and I feel great all day." She went on to say, "In fact, I take my dog and when we finish I have a shower and get to work feeling really positive!'

One of the other delegates responded, "It's alright for you but I haven't got a dog!"

You can imagine the fun I've had recounting this story over the years. But what a great example of giving a reason why something can't be done.

So, when we use reasons, or we are blaming someone or something else, we are not taking responsibility, but we may not be aware of it.

The term 'cause and effect', with assigned boxes, is generally used in NLP. If you are at cause, you are taking responsibility and driving your own bus. If you are in the effects box, you are blaming something or someone else.

There are only two boxes; the cause box is the box you are in when you are driving the bus. The effects box is where you are when you are using excuses, reasons or blaming something or someone else. Here's the killer, you can only be in one or the other. It is digital, on or off, not half in, half out!

I find this useful in a number of ways. Firstly, if I'm not in a great state, which box am I in? That's right, the effects box. And what do I do to get myself into a positive state? Ask myself a 'better question'! For example, "What result do I want?" or "What action can I take?"

Another way of expressing the cause and effect tool, which some people prefer is above the line or below the line.

If you are above the line, you are taking:
Ownership
Accountability
Responsibility

If you are below the line, you are using:
Blame
Excuses
Denial

Easy to remember, OAR and BED. And there's more! Whenever you are above the line your emotions will be positive, you will have a can-do attitude, you will be flourishing. Conversely, when you are below the line, you will possibly have a can't-do attitude and you will be feeling one or more negative emotions and using outside-in thinking.

The above the line concept is very useful to teach to the person you are coaching and to show to your team. It is vital that the coachee takes personal responsibility, for only then does the coaching begin.

"There is an expiry date on blaming your parents for steering you in the wrong direction; the moment you are old enough to take the wheel, responsibility lies with you." J. K. Rowling

Chapter Ten—Leadership

An Idea for a New Book on Leadership

Andy Cope and I were in the pub yesterday (I know, it was 2 p.m. in the afternoon and you are not supposed to do that anymore). We were discussing ideas for a new book on leadership. Generally, these titles are between 80,000 and 120,000 (very big) words.

We had only had one pint each. Here is what we came up with:

Once upon a time, there was a leader who spent lots of face-to-face time with her team. She delegated stuff to them so that they could grow their confidence and capability, and coached them to come up with their own solutions. Every day, she reminded them why they were doing what they were doing and painted the big picture. Everyone needs a purpose! She got them involved with team decisions and treated them as she would like to be treated. She had bags of energy and enthusiasm, which rubbed off. And she bought lots of cakes, but not necessarily on a Friday.

And she was the best leader ever.

THE END

"My job was to make everyone understand that the impossible was possible. That's the difference between leadership and management." Sir Alex Ferguson

So, how does NLP impact on leadership? If you are in an upbeat positive mood, if you are confident, if you set and achieve goals, you will inspire others... or, will you? What if it is not true that we can inspire others? What if people can only inspire themselves? What if people can only become inspired when they *decide* to be?

The trick is, how can you facilitate that happening? Behaviour breeds behaviour, so they may consciously and unconsciously copy your actions and behaviours. I think delegating and coaching are key tools you can use. I'm absolutely convinced that you, the leader or coach, have to believe that the person you are working with has that flame inside them which I'll describe as a 'seam of gold' shortly. Remember, you are the one who turns their light switch on, but they already have the potential energy inside them. Kim Cameron advocates leaders having positive relationships, which furthers his concept of 'positive deviation' in which teams flourish, bringing the organisation success. Positive relationships reduce stress levels and impact on health and wellbeing. Daniel Goleman suggests that where leaders are positive and emotionally intelligent this translates to bottom line results.

It's worth exploring how coaching can be used in leadership and some other approaches you can use to get results.

Time for a bit of theory. After reading it you can go and lie down in a dark room for half an hour until you are fully recovered! Big, deep breath, here we go.

There are several leadership models which utilise coaching as a leadership style or behaviour. However, the role of coaching by a leader will involve being clear about your team member's role and area of responsibility. The executive coach and author, Mary Beth O'Neil, suggests that there are two roles for the leader to perform:

1. Communicate your expectations to your team member and ensure that they commit to them.
2. Coach and develop your team member to accomplish those expectations.

64

In the 1970s, Ken Blanchard and Paul Hersey introduced the 'Situational Leadership' model. They proposed that effective leaders would adapt their approach, selecting between four styles based on the employee's competence, motivation and confidence. This is a very practical and functional tool. Not only can you adapt your style to suit the situation, but you can also use it to map out where your team generally sit across the level of development and corresponding styles. However, it could be argued that this model is dated in its view of coaching, described as being more directive, such as the way a sports coach instructs a player on how to do something.

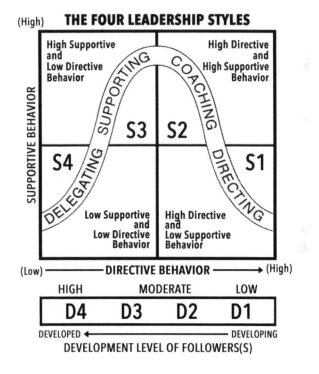

The styles S1-S4 correspond to the employee's development levels D1-D4. Supportive behaviour means being there with the team member and investing time in their development, whereas, Directing S1 implies instruction, telling them what to do and how to do it. In S2 you still tell them what to do and how to do it, but explain *why* it is being done and the impact on other teams and people. It provides the employee with the big picture and the *why* of the task, which is vital. Too many people do not understand where what they do fits in with the wider organisation and how important their contribution is.

TIP — Sit down with your team members and check their understanding of *why* they are doing a particular task and whom it impacts.

The coaching we subscribe to occurs in S3 and S4, where the leader lets go but keeps an eye on things. In S3 the leader delegates the task to a degree, but keeps an eye on the situation. For example, they may delegate the production of a monthly board report to a team member, but ask to look over it before it is distributed. A project manager is generally operating in S3 when they conduct project review meetings, getting updates on progress and the project plan. The model is very useful for any leader because of its flexible approach. In team development we would expect to see movement from S2 to S3 and S4 as the leader paints a picture of the outcome and explains why the task is important, then delegates some responsibility and decision-making (S3), whilst keeping an eye on the situation and then finally delegating full responsibility using the S4 style.

S1 is good because people feel they are contributing straight away. If you give them a simple task to do, it will get them motivated and involved. You tell them what to do and how to do it. This may occur before you sit down with them and do a team or company induction, or explain a more complex task. I would not generally use S1 with new starters because I think it is important to spend time with them explaining things.

With S2 it is important to explain *why* we are doing something a certain way, but its approach is still quite directive because you are telling them why they are doing something and what and how to do it. It is high on support because you are there with them. An example would be when my son Josh gets home from school and I ask if he has any homework, he might reply, "Yeah, maths."

I say, "Let's sit down and look at the question after dinner."

At S3, we are still supportive but beginning to let go. With a subject he is strong in, such as English or History, I might say, "give me a shout if you want to run anything past me." S3 is where you are keeping an eye on things, so people can ask you for support, or when you know they are at a higher risk stage in a project.

S4 is all about delegating. So why delegate? The answer is that delegation grows people around you and it develops new leaders for your organisation. It frees you up to take on more responsibility and have time to think about developing your area. The situational leadership model gives a route to progress people. When you first take your child to the swimming pool you hold them in their rubber ring. Then, as they get older and more confident, you let go and let them paddle towards you, whilst encouraging and keeping a close eye on them. Then the arm bands come off and you stay close, ready to hold them if needed, as they learn to swim. You keep a close eye on them, but as they develop you can keep less of an eye on them until they can do it safely on their own.

Some managers don't like to delegate because they think they can do it quicker themselves. Or perhaps it's because they have got into a habit of doing certain tasks on their own. I believe that quite a few managers, who are very directive, have a fear of something going wrong. The problem with being too directive is that team members are being denied the opportunity to grow, and can become restricted, forever having to ask what is required and how it is to be done. It is like planting a tree in a small pot. Eventually they will leave, or stay and whither. If you take over a team where people are used to being told what to do, you may have to be patient and encourage them with small steps.

Delegating an area of responsibility then periodically coaching the person can be rewarding for both parties.

An effective leader will use all four styles. Sometimes, if an employee's motivation drops, a leader may switch from S4 to S2 and focus the team member on their objectives. They may also monitor progress more closely.

Situational leadership can apply to the management of suppliers and other stakeholders. Some of your suppliers will be reliable and understand your requirements, so you can have a hands-off approach, whilst others will require closer monitoring.

Bernard Bass continued the work others had started on transformational leadership, in which the leader displays four behaviours or approaches. He argued that the leader serves as a role model, with the right behaviours and values by walking the talk. They articulate a "compelling vision", they encourage innovation and creativity, approaching old problems in new ways and they coach and mentor team members. These four behaviours can be either participative or directive. For example, the leader could set the vision and communicate it, or they could share the development of the vision with their team.

The term transactional leadership (or management) is used to describe the more traditional management practices, such as budgeting, planning and control. The current thinking and research demonstrates that the transactional approach will not get the best from people.

In our leadership training, delegates usually want to develop their coaching/delegating styles.

Daniel Goleman, whose work on emotional intelligence is renowned, developed a model for leadership with Richard Boyatis and Annie McGee. 'Goleman's Repertoire' is made up of six styles:

Visionary, which involves the leader creating a strategy and vision with the team.

Coaching, which includes delegating. The leader uses coaching as a leadership style, delegating and coaching the team member.

Democratic, where decision-making is shared with the team, e.g. in team meetings or a similar setting.

Affiliative, which means both working in the team to produce results together, and having a social awareness or empathy with the group. The leader is attuned to the moods in the team, and, when the team is busy, the leader gets stuck in and works alongside them.

These four styles all create a positive resonance in the group, which leads to bottom line improvements and profitability, rather like the positive deviance championed by Kim Cameron.

The two other styles within 'Goleman's Repertoire' are:

Pace Setting, which is useful in small doses but can create unnecessary pressure because it involves the leader continually asking for updates on progress.

Commanding, which borders on bullying.

Both these styles create dissonance or disharmony within the team. Simon Sinek says that, when we feel threatened, we produce cortisol, which results in stress, anxiety and a lack of trust. The pace setting style is often used by middle managers who are expediting work, for example service engineers responding to callouts for repair may be continually called by their manager to see if they are at the next customer yet. Pace setting will eventually wear down an employee and impact on their performance.

So, how do you know which style to use or even which model? You can judge how competent someone is so you can work out how much responsibility to give them in a particular area, then you can coach them as they progress. Create a vision with your team and involve them in decision-making where you can. Both transformational leadership and 'Goleman's Repertoire' fit with the spirit of NLP, which encourages personal responsibility and growth, and enables people to transform themselves and the wider community, which includes their organisations. Both require lots of energy from the leader. It can't be done by sitting in your office writing emails!

Effective leaders spend time with their people; they are energetic and avoid delegating with messenger or email.

Anthropologists suggest that humans began to walk on two legs so that they could use their arms for carrying food. Their gluteal muscles became the largest muscle in the body as they evolved to run and hunt and cover large distances. I guess what I'm saying is that, as a leader, your bottom was not intended for sitting on at your desk!

The Hotel Manager and Leadership

"There he goes again!" exclaimed one of our delegates on the NLP Practitioner course last week.

As we watched out of the window, John, the General manager, was wheeling out a laundry basket on his way to see the site engineer of the company constructing 19 new bedrooms and a new floor for the hotel. He moves quickly. This morning I saw him collecting an empty tray from the breakfast buffet, whilst on the way to the kitchen to check on numbers.

It's not just the small stuff, he does the big things too. Revenue is up, and room occupation, too. They built a new restaurant last year and new bedrooms. Staff turnover is low. His longest serving employee Giovanni retired in the spring, after 47 years. We saw him conducting two one-to-ones yesterday. So, what is his approach to leadership? This is what I have seen:

1. He has a close attention on detail and maintains standards.

2. He spends a lot of time with customers and has a great rapport.

3. He is on the floor nearly all the time and helps the staff.

4. He has a vision for the hotel and has overseen its expansion and profitability.

5. He has huge personal energy.

This sums it up – and it's all transferable wherever you work.

Chapter Eleven — Ethics and Values

Simon Sinek in *Leaders Eat Last*, talks about the differences between being legal and moral. He uses the example of the number of lifeboats on the Titanic, which was above the legal requirement at the time but a small proportion of what was required when the ship sank.

We have major corporations, who have huge sales in the UK, but use legal tax avoidance schemes. Some argue that this creates unfair competition, others maintain that they are within the regulations. In recent years, Mid Staffordshire NHS Hospital Trust was accused of neglecting patients suggesting an absence of the leadership behaviours espoused by Bass. Volkswagen was thought to be falsifying emissions tests, which could cost them billions of dollars. If ever there was a case for senior leadership integrity and honesty the VW emissions case demonstrates it with hard cash numbers.

Your values will be your own compass and the foundation of your decision-making. Some leaders deviate from their values, principals and beliefs because of pressure put upon them by others. A lower level limiting belief and an unconscious need for security can make it difficult to stay aligned to personal values. But, once you get rid of limiting beliefs, it will be easier to do the right thing. Whatever that is for you.

The Beliefs Which Successful Leaders and Coaches Hold

I am going to introduce a set of beliefs and values which successful leaders and coaches hold. If you pick up another book on NLP or go on a practitioner course you will come across the term NLP presuppositions, which just means the assumptions or beliefs we hold about the people we are leading and coaching.

Have respect for another person's model of the world. We adopt the attitude that other people have received different things through their filters and, therefore, have a different script, the question is, how can you communicate with them?

This applies to the people you interact with, not necessarily terrorists, before you ask, though you may wonder what drives and motivates them and query their values levels. Nor does it apply to Man City fans, or people who open their car door against yours and dent it in the Tesco car park.

Some of my delegates argue that accepting that other people have a different model of the world is a good starting point in understanding their point of view. In other words, you don't have to respect what they are saying, just accept that they are different. Others argue that having respect for another's model of the world or script is correct, whatever it is.

When coaching, you will be challenging the coachee's model of the world or their script. I don't advocate making suggestions when I teach coaching, because the coach's questions will be based on their own model of the world and, here is a scary thought, you could actually be limiting your coachee because of your model of the world and your own limiting beliefs.

When you are coaching someone, and assisting them in setting goals, then **check that the outcome fits with their wider values** and, ultimately, is for good for the wider environment or system.

Resistance from someone you are communicating with may be due to a lack of rapport. Try changing the way you communicate and understand their model of the world and values. Remember the story of my delegate who changed her approach with her teenage daughter? Before she was facing resistance, but now their relationship has changed.

People are not their behaviours. If we have an opinion about someone, our doorman and filters will target the behaviours that support our opinion. Revisiting an earlier example, a manager may be too directive, not delegating enough and lack some emotional intelligence, and some may say he is a poor manager! But, by being aware that we generalise, we will have a completely different mind-set if we accept the person and help them work on their behaviours.

So, if you call your boyfriend an idiot that is not good, however, you can say, "you are acting like an idiot."

Everyone is doing the best they can with the resources they have available to them. Workshop delegates often contest this, and they could be right. However, I interpret resources as a person's values, beliefs and model of their world. An everyday example of this is of a colleague who gets nervous before doing a presentation. They are doing the best they can. You, the coach or leader, can build their confidence or do some simple NLP techniques. (See Limiting Belief Change and SWISH Pattern in a later chapter.)

The most important information about someone is their behaviour. The example I might use for this is when you are coaching someone, and you meet for a follow up session a couple of months later and they have not taken any action. What they say they want to achieve is less important than what they actually do. Coaching is not really coaching unless action plans are followed through.

We are in charge of our mind and, therefore, our results. There are environmental factors which influence our outcomes, but using positive self-talk, monitoring your thoughts and being aware of your negativity bias will stack the odds in your favour. If you put the right stuff into your mind and take action you are more likely to achieve something. And, if you are not getting the result you want, you can choose how you respond to that and flex your behaviour. This leads us nicely onto the next one.

Have the ability to be more flexible in your behaviour. The more flexible you can be in your approach, the more likely you are to achieve a better result. Often when you change your approach to someone you get a more rewarding outcome. The same applies to the way you do your job. If you are running a coaching business and you are not getting enough clients maybe it's time to think about other ways of marketing. Test them out, but don't be too concerned if a method does not work. It is about testing and measuring until you discover a methodology or methodologies that work.

People have all the resources they need to succeed and to achieve their desired outcomes. This is basically saying that no one lacks resourcefulness, but they can have states which lack resources e.g. when someone is below the line. I would also add that it is important to play to people's strengths. Developing people around their strengths instils confidence and people are happier doing tasks they enjoy. It will encourage them to develop further in a particular field or vocation.

There is only feedback! There is no failure, only feedback. It's just a result. If you think you may fail at something you possibly won't attempt it and certainly will not approach it with certainty and conviction. Fear of failure holds many people back from stretching their comfort zones and taking on a new goal or opportunity. However, when you see every outcome as a result, you are maintaining a more resourceful state and increasing your chances of success.

Communication is not effective if you don't get a response or some action. You are responsible for communicating effectively so that others understand. How many times have you heard someone ask, "did you get my email?" And they expect you to have taken some action.

All coaching interventions should offer more options for the coachee. Your role as a coach is to challenge their model of the world and current thinking, whilst assisting them in developing their options.

Chapter Twelve — Emotional Intelligence

The Emotional Intelligence Lift —
A Little Story on Emotional Intelligence
(Based on a concept by Sydney Banks)

Every day, when our leader looked out of the office window, he would see the parked cars and delivery vehicles loading for their next drop. His mind recorded the scene like a video camera. As he walked through the office he could sense the mood. Something had happened. He was good at tuning in to his team and other colleagues. He had learned to notice small changes in their physiology, which supported his own intuition. He asked a few questions, acknowledging the problem and asked what ideas they had. Soon, his team were focused on some possible positive solutions and the usual energy was back.

Sometime later, he became involved with a call from an irate customer. As was the procedure, his team would escalate these to him. When the customer started shouting down the line his instinct was to become defensive, he could feel the emotion beginning to rise.

He stepped into his emotional elevator. Through the window, on the ground floor, his mind recorded the situation (as he saw it). As the lift began to rise, the view began to blur a little, now he could see not only the customers perspective, but also other perspectives on the situation. When he got to the 30th floor, the view became more like a painting, with the images swirling and changing. He could see different solutions unfolding. The issue was soon resolved.

THE END

Do you know what impact you are having on other people?
Do events or people ever make you angry or upset? If a car

79

pulls out into your lane on the motorway without indicating, does it irritate you or do you feel calm and let it ride?

Often people are not consciously aware that they get angry, upset or irritated until they get feedback from someone else or are made aware of the concept of emotional intelligence (EI). Many delegates on our leadership training have made significant progress in developing their EI. We have had comments from their colleagues about them being a "changed man".

According to Daniel Goleman, the impact of a significant emotional event can result in anger being triggered a few days later, by a different event, which is low in significance and would not usually be an issue. I found this useful in understanding why I was letting something fairly trivial upset me.

At one time, people were measured only by their intelligence quotient (IQ), which is fine if you want to be an academic. The professor who is conducting a lecture to one hundred students won't even notice if some of the students are walking out. He will carry on, immersed in his subject. Whereas the restaurant manager will be conscious of a table of guests who have gone quiet or want attention. The customer service manager will empathise with the customer, whilst managing the situation.

Howard Gardner identified multiple intelligences, such as bodily-kinaesthetic intelligence; the ability to control one's body movements and handle objects skilfully, in which footballers or tennis players become adept. He also identified intrapersonal intelligence; the ability to be self-aware of one's own feeling and emotions, and interpersonal intelligence; to be aware of others' emotions and motivation and to be able to respond accordingly.

The four elements of emotional intelligence identified by Daniel Goleman are:

Self-Awareness — feeling upset or angry is usually the result of an emotional reaction as opposed to a rational response. It can also mean being conscious of your thoughts. Remember, our feelings are a barometer for our thoughts, which means that we can begin to start the process of self-managing our thought and feelings.

Self-Management — a question you can ask yourself is, "will this really matter in six months?"

When we become consciously aware of our thoughts we can choose our response, as opposed to reacting. When we do this, we are building new neural pathways in the brain and eroding old habits.

Social Awareness — means having empathy and being attuned to group feelings. The example in the story demonstrates how our leader was aware of the mood in his team.

Social Management — being able to manage the situation and take people with you.

Emotional Intelligence can be developed by growing new neurological pathways and hard-wiring new behaviours. Let's take the emotion of anger, because that is where most people struggle, even if it is only with irritation.

First of all, we have our fight or flight response. A direct signal containing some of the information about a perceived threat goes straight to the amygdala or the limbic area of our brain. This enables fight or flight and will produce lots of chemicals in our body to give us energy. This signal happens far quicker than the time it takes for our neocortex to process the information in order for us to formulate a rational response. So, we may irrationally react

81

to someone because of a perceived threat or injustice. Caveman Kev kicking in with his 'Corrie' glasses on.

We also learn to 'do' anger from a very early age, when we cry as a baby because we are hungry that is the only way we can communicate our need. If we could talk at the age of two weeks we would say, "Mum, where are you? I'm hungry."

New neuron pathways develop every time we get angry until there is a clear pathway or channel which we automatically follow when some event or person triggers it. It is similar to Pavlov's Dogs experiment. Pavlov rang a bell and showed the dogs a steak, and they salivated. He repeated this many times, then he just rang the bell (no steak) and the dogs still salivated.

So, the strong pathway of learned behaviour develops, the only way to change it is to be consciously aware of when the trigger occurs and interrupt the pattern with something like a question or something you say to yourself such as:

Trigger Event 1 — The car in front of you keeps slowing down.
"I bet that driver is lost or looking for an address which is why she keeps slowing down", or "perhaps it's an elderly person and they are lacking confidence".

Trigger Event 2 — You are concentrating whilst working at home and your phone rings, it's a number you don't recognise, but you decide to pick it up just in case. However, it's a cold call and you could get irritated and hang up or you could say to yourself:

"I bet he is on a low wage and doing his best to feed his family." You politely say that you are not interested and inform him you are telephone preference service registered and could he update his records? You will feel calm and happy.

The good news is that the more you keep consciously choosing your response, the more the old pathway will reduce in its automatic reaction.

Stay with it, sometimes you will fail but that's okay, it takes time and effort.

As in the earlier example, based on Sydney Banks' suggestion, we can raise our awareness or consciousness by imagining we are in a lift. On the lower floors we feel in conflict and don't see the other person's point of view, but as we elevate to the higher levels in our imagination we see the event from a different perspective. This will also facilitate the growth of our neurology. The chapter on value levels explains how our values evolve through neurological development. Our awareness or levels of consciousness will support this growth.

TIP—Be aware of your feelings, a negative feeling is the result of a thought, so if you think about an event differently, you can choose your response and get a positive outcome. Inside-out thinking delineates emotional intelligence and provides a simple method of developing it.

Once the neuron pathways develop, the negative emotion can operate in different contexts over a person's life. One woman I was coaching felt resentment about her mother-in-law. Once she thought about the feelings, i.e. being conscious, the feeling of resentment seemed to disappear. I asked her if there were any other areas in life where she felt resentment. We ended up with quite a list, she resented living in a terrace house because she felt she should be doing better, she resented a colleague because the colleague did not focus his effort on sales, or so my coachee thought. Incidentally, a week after my coachee became conscious of this, her colleague identified a potential new client and had sent them a proposal. What was interesting, she revealed, was that, when she thought about it, the feeling of resentment had started some fifteen years earlier. Her first boyfriend, who was in the forces, returned home from Germany and would spend a lot of time with his mum and dad. She realised that, because of her own insecurities, she resented this.

It seems that once we become conscious of a negative emotion, we can let it go, providing we accept that the emotion is our responsibility and not caused by someone or something else.

Acknowledging the concept of 'outside thinking', where you think your feelings come from external events, rather than your own thinking, is really empowering for managing your state. Inside-out thinking occurs when you accept that your feelings come from your thoughts, therefore, if you recognise that it is just a thought, then you will be able to self-manage your emotion. Or swap from your Coronation Street glasses to a pair which serve you better. I'll let you name your own.

Your Impact as a Leader

Who in your organisation leaves you feeling good when you meet them? What do they do and how do they do it? If you have ever watched the TV programme *Take Me Out* you know that when the guy comes out of the love lift Paddy will say to the girls, "No likey, no lighty". The women will

84

turn off their light if they don't like the look of the poor bloke. But what is all this to do with leadership? I sometimes say to leaders at conferences. "When you come down the love lift at the start of your day, do your team leave their lights on or do they turn them off?"

We have all heard, and forgotten, that first impressions count. Steve McDermott suggested that in the first four minutes of meeting someone they make up their mind about you. He developed the four-minute rule, which involves a 'better question' you can ask yourself prior to the event, as it immediately changes your state.

If you are a parent, ask yourself, what would the best mum or dad in the world look like, act like and feel like, before you walk in at night, you will instantly feel happy and your child will be the focus of your attention. Or, what would the best (insert your job title) in the world look like act like and feel like? Our delegates say that when they do this, they spend more time walking the floor with their teams, getting to know the little things about them. Richard, a manager of one of our customers, said that his shift supervisors stopped bombarding him with problems the moment he walked in and, instead, started solving problems themselves. Ben, at a council, taught it to his managers and supervisors, and the staff survey on key questions about leadership went from 28% to 85% the following year.

TIP—Before you go into work, ask yourself, what would the best (insert job title) look like act like and feel like?

Chapter Thirteen — Coaching in Business

Let's face it, you can't motivate other people. You may be inspired and inspirational, but they have to decide to motivate themselves. The experts call it intrinsic motivation. Once someone has decided to be motivated you can begin coaching. That is when the real energy starts to flow.

Society and the business environment are rapidly changing. In organisations, people are required to be more self-reliant and work across a spectrum of teams and stakeholders. Often, they are working away from a central office with a variety of people who may even belong to other organisations. Traditional hierarchies are being replaced by ever-changing project teams and structures.

People no longer work for a gold watch, they don't want others controlling their destiny. We are moving from a structured, 'know your place' society into one where people want to express their independence. More people than ever before are moving into self-employment, managers can no longer rely on measuring presentism, they will have to focus on output as more employees work from home. Several organisations we work with have teams being managed across international borders. This means we need leaders who can build rapport and trust, who delegate and inspire.

Delegating and growing people through coaching is more cost-effective than recruiting new people into leadership positions. Sir John Whitmore suggested that coaching unlocks people's potential to maximise their performance. It is estimated that an employee costs some 50% on top of their salary to employ them when we take into account national insurance, holidays, IT and HR support, office space and equipment. To have an asset who is not providing a return on investment is wasteful and uncompetitive, and not fair on them either.

So, what is coaching and how does it differ from mentoring? Sir John Whitmore describes coaching as a process of helping people learn, rather than teaching them. Coaching is all about raising someone's awareness so that they can take responsibility for driving their own bus. Coaching stimulates individuality; it empowers employees to take responsibility and take action to achieve organisational goals.

Myles Downey, a renowned business coach, has developed the 'push pull' concept, which shows a continuum of behaviours, ranging from telling and teaching, to asking the coachee questions.

I have a theory that you can't push string. Only the coachee can pull it!

'Non-directive' coaching facilitates the coachee into discovering their own solutions. According to Myles Downey, this is where the magic occurs, and I agree.

Coaching or Mentoring?

I am sometimes asked to define the differences between coaching and mentoring. Some people use the term coaching and mentoring interchangeably. Some writers define mentoring as a longer relationship with a more experienced person. I guess you can compare a mentor to Yoda. Sir John Whitmore states that true coaching takes the coachee beyond the limitations of the coach's knowledge. Coaches don't have to have knowledge of the field they are coaching, though it may help them ask the right questions. However, having a limited knowledge of the coachee's field may require the coach to ask basic questions to understand the coachee's situation. Such questioning raises the awareness and options for the coachee. At this point I would strongly suggest that you, as a coach, do not give examples from your own experience to show empathy. It is about your coachee, not you.

In professional coaching practice we don't offer advice or tell the coachee what to do. Coaching concentrates the coachee on the best strategies to achieve their desired outcomes. The role of the coach is to help the coachee or client discover where their process and thinking is going wrong and then correct it. It is about challenging their model of the world and helping them fit a new pair of glasses.

As I suggested before, you could limit your coachee by your own limiting beliefs and your own model of the world, which is another reason not to make suggestions. Consider this, if you are making suggestions you may be formulating plans in your mind about actions the coachee could take, if you are doing this you will *not* be listening to what the coachee is saying, instead you will be pushing your own agenda.

The mentoring of junior and middle managers may involve answering questions such as, "how do I get noticed and promoted?", whereas an executive might be asking how they can develop or build a leadership team or "What do I want from my life/career?".

Mentoring usually involves a longer-term relationship, whereas coaching is a shorter-term relationship to achieve specific outcomes and learning.

The mentor will usually have knowledge and experience to impart. Mentoring of senior people requires the mentor to have a strong understanding of business, ideally from having had success in a similar role. The mentor may still use coaching questions to challenge the mentee. They may offer advice or disclose similar situations from their own career. When I started my first session with someone who was starting their own business, I asked them if they wanted me to mentor or coach them. They wanted a mentor and we identified areas of opportunity they could market themselves in and how much they would have to charge for their services.

Mentoring can be informal, between older friends or through work relationships.

Coaching to Get Results!

I remember a great story from American guru, Zig Ziglar. Apparently, at the beginning of the twentieth century, a Texan farmer had to put his land up for sale because he was struggling to make a living. An oil company approached him and offered him a royalty on every barrel of oil if they could drill on his land. The farmer had nothing to lose and the drilling started. Zig goes on to say that a gusher came out and it made the farmer an instant millionaire. Or did it? Zig has this terrific way of making you think. Could it have been that the farmer was a millionaire before they struck black gold? He was sitting on an untapped fortune. He just didn't know it.

Applying the same principle to people... perhaps we already have all the resources we need. What potential riches and strengths are we sitting on which are waiting to be tapped into? And it's not just about you! What about the potential of the people in your workplace?

Why Coach with NLP?

Sir John Whitmore quotes Timothy Gallwey from his book *The Inner Game of Tennis.* "The opponent within one's own head is more formidable than the one on the other side of the net." Throughout Whitmore's book *Coaching for Performance,* he makes references to concepts, questioning techniques and self-belief that the field of NLP can facilitate. Coaching provides a great process to which we can apply the NLP toolbox.

NLP and Coaching are all about tapping into reserves we already have. Companies spend a fortune on recruiting new talent, when coaching could grow your existing in-house people.

The Pygmalion Principle

Before we discuss the Pygmalion principle I would like to share with you another of Zig's stories. Zig recalls an interview between a newspaper correspondent and Andrew Carnegie, a great industrialist in the late nineteenth and early twentieth century. Apparently, the journalist discovered that Carnegie had 38 millionaires working for him. The reporter asked why he had hired 38 millionaires.

"They were not millionaires when I hired them," Carnegie replied. The journalist asked what he had done to make the men so valuable that he could pay them so much. Carnegie replied, "When you are mining for gold, you are looking for the seam of gold."

The key here is for your coachee or team member to realise that they have a seam of gold or that potential energy or electricity already inside them. The Pygmalion

Principle is based upon a quote from the play, which was later made into the musical and film *My Fair Lady*, in which Professor Higgins has a bet with his friend Colonel Pickering that he could take an East End flower girl and pass her off as a lady. As the film develops, to paraphrase, Eliza remarks to Pickering that the Professor still sees her as a flower girl who has changed her behaviours, but, to Pickering, she is a lady!

In other words, the coach has to see the seam of gold within the coachee. Good teachers do the same. Parents know that their child will be able to do things if they encourage them. Encouragement is a marvellous word, the Oxford English Dictionary defines it as "the action of giving someone support, confidence, or hope".

We were doing some leadership training with primary school head teachers and deputy head teachers. One group was discussing a particular local head teacher, whom they said had an amazing ability to "see the seam of gold" in others.

"How do you think she does it?" they asked me.

I thought for a moment and answered, "Perhaps she expects it to be there, so she sees it."

The more I thought about it afterwards, the more confident I was that this was true. Indeed, it's the 'Doorman' allowing information in.

A few months later, the very same head teacher from Nottingham, Sharon Gray, won *The Pride of Britain Award*. Having worked with a number of her team I can see evidence of her other leadership qualities and innovative approach. It is all about believing people have that 'seam of gold', expecting to find it and giving them responsibility and ownership. And boy, do Sharon's team shine and burst with enthusiasm!

The Coaching Process

I base my sessions around the GROW model, which is used extensively by coaches. There are other models, but I find this the most straightforward. Before we start, there will be some kind of contract in place, which can be a simple verbal agreement or more formal. If you are a professional coach, your 'client' is the organisation who pays you, not necessarily your coachee. It is important to agree, with all concerned, what will and what will not be disclosed to whom.

The GROW Model

G	Goal
R	Reality check — where are they now?
O	Options — what options do they have?
W	Will — do they really want to achieve this goal? The coachee needs to do the work.

Goal

The process may involve assisting the coachee in identifying a few clear goals. Sometimes, they are not sure what they want. Often big picture or chunked up (see section on rapport) questions are used with more detailed questions to clarify the coach's understanding. As this dialogue progresses we will move towards more specific and measurable outcomes. The goal should be specific, and it must be possible to measure whether it has been achieved. Having identified the goal, questions like "How will you know that you have achieved that goal?", are useful and enable us to measure success.

If you have to assist the coachee in establishing a goal, there are numerous ways of exploring what they want. It might be based on a financial outcome they want to achieve or an aspect of their life that isn't being fulfilled. The section on values will help facilitate this process.

Reality

As well as knowing where you are trying to get to, you need to know where you are starting from – the current reality. Sir John Whitmore believes that it is surprising how often this is the key part of a coaching session, and by seeing the situation clearly, (rather than what was thought or imagined to be the situation), the resolution becomes obvious and straightforward. When a goal has not been established, or when I want to clarify and understand what the coachee wants, I start with 'reality' questions.

Options

Once you know where you are and where you want to go, the next step is to explore what options you have for getting there. A metaphor for GROW is a map; once you know where you are going (the goal), and where you are (the current reality), you can explore possible ways of making the journey (options) and choose the best. It is useful to recognise the language the coachee employs to notice if they are limiting their options. If they are blaming someone else or using *reasons*, you can ask chunked down questions (see language and rapport sections) to uncover the meaning of what the coachee is saying. The coachee may also limit their options; "I can do one thing or another", limiting their choices. You can counter with "what other options might be available?" This is an example of the coach asking questions to challenge the coachee's model of the world.

The language section explains, in detail, how we can recognise these language patterns in business, coaching and life in general.

Will

I am concerned that, on occasion, people might see coaching as 'a bit of a talking shop'. For example, the Finance Director who is approving your budget would be right to challenge the return on investment, which is why every coach should make measurement a priority.

It is wise to coach someone who has a goal or a business need so that we can measure return on investment and estimate conservatively the percentage that was due to the coaching sessions. Of course, development needs will emerge too.

I told the Andrew Carnegie gold-mining story to a group of delegates on a leadership programme a few years ago and one responded, "So, the coach asks the questions, but the coachee has to do the shovelling of the soil to get to the gold?"

That's a perfect definition of will. The coachee has to be above the line and take action!

I insist that if the coachee has an idea they write it down immediately, which seems to cement it and make it more real to them. You can tell from their tone of voice becoming more determined when they get a meaningful realisation.

At the end of the session, the coachee should have written out an action plan with the names of people they are going to involve and timescales. The coach should make a copy of this so that they can follow it up. In two months' time you will not remember if they were going to talk with Rebecca or Lena. Some coaches will draw a mind map of the session or take notes; you have to find your own balance but having a record means that you can refresh your memory before you meet them for another session.

Follow Up Sessions

The follow up should be after an agreed period, so that the coachee has been able to make progress. There is no point in making them weekly unless there is a specific reason and you can justify the time in achieving their objective. The duration between sessions will be based on what has been agreed in the contract. A good professional coach will not 'hang on' to the coachee for too long, otherwise they become dependent on each other. In some circumstances both may decide to follow up on an annual basis.

Questions

Many people who learn to coach struggle not to give the coachee solutions or they will ask leading questions that give very strong clues to the action that they think the coachee should take. Remember, if you try to lead the coachee down a path that you think they should go then this is based on your model of the world and, possibly, your own limiting beliefs.

These leading questions will not allow the coachee to have as much ownership for the solutions and actions they are developing into a plan. As I mentioned, Myles Downey suggests that when the coachee is working things out for themselves this is where the magic occurs.

If I feel a coachee is struggling, I will ask, "Who is the most effective person you know?" Then I ask, "What would they do in this situation?"

I don't know how it happens, I can only conclude it is their unconscious mind, but every time they have a solution. And then I might leave it there and let them ponder and dwell on a course of action, or I would ask, "Is that something you *might* consider doing?" They invariably say yes. Note, the language I use is quite soft.

Too Much Talking!

The coachee does the talking and the reflecting. There will be silences and that's okay, the coachee is processing. Yes, the coach can ask questions to uncover the coachee's deletions, distortions and generalisations, and for the coachee to understand the situation better. (See language section.)

The GROW model enables us to use big picture, chunked up questions to establish goals and direction for the coachee, and chunked down questions to understand their thinking and challenge their model of the world.

The Business Benefits of Coaching

As we have said, recruiting from outside your organisation is expensive and comes with risks. It is less expensive to coach someone from within in order for them to develop, so that they are ready when a promotion or new opportunity arises. The cost of recruiting is expensive, often 20% of the first year's salary, and can be risky if it does not work out.

Why does coaching work? At the end of each coaching session there should be a list of actions that the coachee has identified. Some of these actions may take the coachee out of their comfort zone, but when they complete them their neurology will develop. When the neurology develops they will no longer be out of their comfort zone if a similar situation arises.

This development occurs throughout our lives. As we move up a year to our new class, we are no longer looking up at the 'big' year six children, we are a year six! As we join the world of employment and our salary increases with a promotion, we think and act at the new level. This is a natural process, what coaching does is accelerate it. Every time new goals and tasks are set and achieved, the neurology develops.

The first time a child rides a bike with stabilisers their brain has not developed enough to balance, however, with practise, and you running along beside them holding the seat, their neurology develops, and they eventually are able to balance.

When you learn to ski you fall over but because you want to ski you get up. While this is happening, your neurology develops to allow you to ski. Imagine your footsteps in the snow each time you walk up the slope (no ski lift). Each step you take in the virgin snow is creating a new path way. When you have done it numerous times there will be lots of footsteps in the snow and the new pathway is created. And, like your footsteps in the snow, new neural pathways are formed.

If the neurology is sufficiently developed, the coachee will be able to respond more positively to changes in their (business) environment. Their comfort zone will be stretched and their new beliefs about themselves will allow the filters to accept new information and possibilities that they did not 'see' previously.

If the coachee's belief and values system are changed through NLP, i.e. we get rid of limiting beliefs, then this provides the confidence to take on new challenges. It is the new goals they set and their subsequent achievement, which develops their neurology. This is why goal setting and achievement is vital in coaching.

In chapter sixteen, we discuss values levels. People can think about being entrepreneurial or taking the plunge to become self-employed, but their neurology is insufficiently developed and they can become frustrated in a predominantly level 4 environment (I'll explain level 4 later). They want to grow, they want to find out about themselves and they want independence.

A number of local authorities in the UK are describing themselves as 'entrepreneurial councils'. However, this is only at their level of thinking, their neurology has not yet developed to be entrepreneurial. This could be achieved by coaching their senior managers, but only when they take action and experience running a business.

Thunderbirds Are Go!

Anyone growing up in the 1960s, 70s or 80s will remember Thunderbirds. *Easter Saturday, saw the return of a revamped* Thunderbirds, *this time with CGI. What I loved about it was the care taken to keep the original DNA, like when Virgil is transported on the slide to Thunderbird 2 there are still jerky movements. I thought Parker looked a bit like Alan Sugar too! Now it's on every Saturday morning on CITV.*

The Tracy brothers, on the other hand, appeared a bit younger, three of them could be the Rice Krispies characters. But, once again, we see personal leadership displayed by them all and very close team work. You don't hear John moaning about being marooned in space on TB5 or Gordon complaining about being underwater again in TB4. They all take on leadership roles depending on the situation. If you still like a sneaky look at Thunderbirds you can say A) I'm bonding with the children, or B) It's about the teamwork! Enjoy!

On the other hand…

Three weeks after originally writing this article I watched a couple of episodes on catch up. Yes, they have great staging and Thunderbird vehicles, but the pace of the programmes is incredibly fast. Possibly, they think eight-year-olds will get bored. No sooner has John received the distress call than TB1 is virtually in situ and the rescue commences. Then there are the acrobatics from Parker and Scott, who climb rocks like Spiderman.

In the original series, the guy in distress would be seen sweating, hanging onto a cliff for 45 minutes as the tension built up, and we loved it. At the end of the hour-long episode we were off out, on our bikes to re-enact the story. These days it's quick action sequences and no suspense. And that brings me to the world of work. Senior managers want action and feed the solutions and suggestions to their team members, instructing them what to do. There is no time available to let them work it out and to learn themselves (with support). Many of us are too busy to coach and too busy to spend time with people.

Chapter Fourteen—Applying NLP Language Patterns in Coaching and Leadership

If you are a professional coach, this chapter will be invaluable. You will be able to read into a person's model of reality from what they are saying. As a leader you will be able to take people with you and understand if they are taking personal responsibility or not.

John Grinder and Richard Bandler developed labels for language patterns based upon transformational grammar, which was created by Noam Chomsky.

On the NLP Practitioner course, we teach these labels for the language patterns and, though they are quite complex, they do help delegates notice the patterns in speech. In this chapter I cover three topic areas that we can use in leadership and coaching. I have chosen some of the more relevant patterns and explained the terminology, sometimes using other, plain English, terms to help you understand their meaning.

Year 2 and 3 Revision

A noun is a name of something or someone.

A verb is a doing word, e.g., Dracula *bites* his victim.

An adverb describes how you do it, e.g., Dracula *slowly* bites his victim.

An adjective modifies a noun, e.g., the *little* test.

We are going to explore three NLP Language tools:

The first is the meta model, which the coach or leader can use to recover information which the speaker (coachee or team member) has deleted, generalised or distorted from their thoughts. The speaker is actually using vague or distorted language and deleting information. In the Milton model, the coach or leader will deliberately use language patterns that are artfully vague so as to elegantly persuade or plant suggestions in the listeners' mind which will be more readily accepted.

In the meta model, the speaker or coachee uses the language patterns (not knowingly of course) and the coach questions their thinking to uncover their meaning, and in the Milton model, the coach uses the patterns to create internal representations and suggestions that are accepted by the listener/s.

The NLP linguistic presuppositions (assumptions) are words that occur in the speaker's sentence, so the coach can be sure that they are hearing correctly and not making assumptions. Secondly, they can be used to detect if the speaker is taking responsibility or does not feel they have choices. Thirdly the leader or coach can ask a question or make a statement, which will move the coachee into a better state by changing their internal representation.

The Meta Model

John Grinder and Richard Bandler developed this by listening to the clients of Virginia Satir. The different types of patterns the clients unknowingly used were classified using the labels from transformational grammar.

In the same way that we delete, distort and generalise information coming in, we do the same when we are converting our thoughts to speech. For example, my son Josh might say, "Do you think *he* (meaning the current striker) is as good as (so and so) was?"

Josh knows who he's talking about, but I have to uncover who it is by asking.

I have grouped the labels into examples of deletions, generalisations and distortions.

Deletions

The first one is where we have turned a process word into a noun. For example, a coachee might say, "We have a poor relationship with that customer." The word "relationship" derives from the process of relating. We ask, "How do you relate to them?"

It makes the coachee conscious of the series of behaviours they are using. People have a tendency to hide behind or use excuses or reasons why something cannot be done or to avoid doing something. As nouns they seem pretty solid, but, here is the thing, they are not. Virginia would ask questions like, "How are you relating to him?", to uncover the deletions, distortions and generalisations they were making.

Here is a list of process words turned into nouns (these are labelled as nominalisations), and examples of responses we can use. Remember, the aim is to uncover what they are saying to give us a better understanding as a leader and to challenge their model of the world if we can.

"There is no *communication* in the council."
What would you like communicating? And by whom?

"We have to do that because of *health and safety*."
Which particular part of the legislation specifies that? Or what might happen if you didn't? Give them choices.

"Our *culture* prevents us from doing that."
What specifically about your culture prevents you? Or what beliefs and behaviours are preventing you?

"*Management* says…"
Which manager?

"The *organisation* believes…"
Who in the organisation?

"The *country* decided it wanted a coalition government."
My favourite. I thought it was individuals that voted, is there a box for them to tick coalition?

"We have a poor *relationship*."
How do you know? How are you relating to them?

Another example of deletions is not specifying the person or thing they are taking about…

"*They don't listen to me.*"
About what? Who does not listen to you?

A comparative deletion means that they are making a statement which is not qualified. For example, "we are better than them."

"*It's expensive.*"
Compared to what?

An unspecified verb does not say how the deed was done. For example, the coachee might say "he *rejected* me", the response should be, "*how* did he reject you?"

With simple deletions, such as *"I'm uncomfortable"*, the response should be "about what or whom?"

Generalisations

Then we have generalisations, such as 'universals'. Universals make one or two things into 'everything', which makes stuff seem bigger than it really is, e.g., everyone, no one, never.

"He can't do anything right."
Really? Nothing?

"There is no communication from HR."
What would you like communicating?

I'll use a term 'modal operators.' These are basically phrases which indicate positive possibility, such as can, will, going to, and phrases which indicate necessity or a lack of choice such as, have to, must do, got to.

When you think about it, the only have tos in life are breathing, sleeping, taking up space, and pretty much everything else is a choice. When we see it as a choice it empowers us and gets us back above the line.

I recall a time when I had a lot of marking to do for groups of delegates doing leadership courses with qualifications. I remember saying to myself, "I have to do all this marking," then I used creative avoidance techniques to put off doing it. After a while, the consequences of my inaction began to form in my mind. "What if the delegates ask where their marks are, and what if their training director asks where they are?" Getting a bit painful now! I got straight back above the line and said to myself, "Mmm,

I sold the programme and I knew there were two assignments and I decided to do the marking. So just shut up and get on with it!"

I find by turning things into choices I take more responsibility and I'm happier doing things I don't like doing and I feel empowered.

In leadership and coaching, the have to, must do and got tos indicate that the coachee is not taking responsibility and may think that they have no choices. They are not driving the bus, in fact they are about to get run over by it!

"I can't find it on the intranet."
Where have you looked?

"I've got to do my appraisals."
Why?
"Because HR said so."
In your own words, what is the purpose of doing appraisals?

Distortions

These occur when someone is 'making it up in their head' based on distorting information to 'fit' with what they believe to be correct based on their script.

The first one is guessing or mind reading, for example:
"He does not like me."
How do you know?

The next category I'm including is cause and effect, which means that someone or something else (not me!) is causing something to happen. And the person speaking is below the line! We call it BSE or blame someone or something else.

"He makes me angry."
How is he making you angry?

"I can't do that because it is above my grade."
What would you do if you were on that grade?

When we are coaching, we can delete, distort and generalise what the other person is saying, so we have to be careful that we are not assuming something. The coachee can do it too. They may distort a situation. Here is an example.

"They don't respect me."
How do you know?

A word of warning… soften your questions otherwise you will lose rapport and sound harsh and uncaring.

The Milton Model

Let me tell you something quite shocking. Milton Erikson NEVER used the Milton model! So, you don't need to either. Well, at least not the names of the labels given to the patterns Richard Bandler and John Grinder heard him using. So, if he can do it, you can too. I suggest that you read it through a few times, remember or learn the examples I have used, and then you can change them to suit your own applications.

Imagine you are in the cinema, it's the latest in the *Superman* series. Suddenly there is a crash from the orchestra, a scream as a woman falls 50 storeys towards the ground, and then a flash of red and blue as *Superman* flies in to save her. Never in a million years would you turn to your companion and say, "I bet they used wires!" What we do instead is suspend our critique. In certain circles this is called 'the critical faculty', the message goes through to the unconscious and bypasses the conscious critique.

When John Grinder and Richard Bandler modelled Milton Erikson they discovered that he used artfully vague language that the conscious mind or 'critical faculty' wouldn't reject.

How can we use Milton language? There are broadly three uses or categories:

First, Milton language is very suggestible and is accepted by the unconscious. There is no critique by the listener.

Secondly, because it is very general and chunked up, a large audience will accept it, though it may have a different meaning to each listener. It is used in marketing, for example, Sky suggests that we "Believe in better".

Thirdly, it can be used to soften what you are saying and also be persuasive.

Richard Bandler and John Grinder used the labels based on transformational linguistics to identify the patterns used by Virginia Satir's clients. What they discovered was that, where Virginia Satir would ask a question to uncover what her client meant, Milton Erikson would use similar vague patterns to bypass the listener's internal critique. Here are some of them used in a business or teaching setting. At the end, I'll show you how I have strung several together in a persuasive/sales situation.

Mind Reads — claiming to know the thoughts or feelings of another.
I know that many of you have had to put a lot of effort in to be here and I understand that you are busy.

108

This shows empathy for the audience.

Lost Performative — these are 'value' judgements, which may include an unspecified comparison.
It's important for leaders to be able to coach.
The person who made the statement has been lost but the listener generally accepts the statement because it makes sense.

Cause and Effect — when it is implied that one thing causes another.
When you complete our NLP Practitioner course you'll become more effective.

Complex Equivalence — where two things are equated to mean the same, or put to you as meaning the same, even if they don't.
Having a new sales director means we can give you a better service.

Presupposition — Linguistic assumption. The listener can assume that what you are saying is correct and that they are not distorting the true meaning.
It's going to be a great year; our sales figures are up.
The words are used in the sentence and imply it's going to be great because the sales figures are up. We'll review more categories of these later and how we can utilise them.

Universal Quantifiers — I like the expression 'allness' and not referring to a specific person or thing.
Everything is wonderful.
All the things…
Everyone is on board!
Everyone can learn everything we're doing today.

All the best companies are recognising that coaching is a powerful tool.
All the best managers use coaching with their teams.

Unspecified Verb (a deletion) — where an adjective or adverb modifier does not specify the verb. Remember Dracula *slowly* (adverb) *bit* his victim.
We are going to succeed.
We are going to wow our staff.
You have not said how, but the listener accepts it.

Tag Question — designed to displace resistance.
Won't you?
It's something that interests you, isn't it?
You've got it now, haven't you?
Does that sound of interest?
It does, doesn't it?

Lack of Referential Index — fails to specify a person or thing, the *object* in the statement is not specified.
One can easily see. It's looking good.

Comparative Deletion — We are not explaining what we are comparing something to.
We're more successful, (than whom?)
Our prices are good value. (Compared to what?)
To revisit the Sky example: *Believe in Better* (better than who or what?). But the slogan suggests that the product; sport, films, etc., is better than their competitors. Each listener will have their own interpretation of what is better.

Pace Current Experience — this just means that I'm reflecting back the experience you are going through.

You're sitting here, listening to me, taking in the information and that means (complex equiv.) that you will have creative ideas about how you can use language yourself.

We use this in the 'yes set' at the end of this section.

Double Bind — two choices, this is very common in selling:

Do you want to start in December or leave it until after the holiday and start in mid January?

Would you like the leadership training with a qualification or without?

Extended Quotes — to displace resistance.

I was talking to the Chief Executive and she said the keynote speaker at the conference stated that successful organisations invest in training during a recession and come out better.

You pick out some senior, credible characters and make a statement, but, in the listener's mind, it appears to have been the conference speaker who made the statement, not you.

Selectional Restrictional Violation — Statements that give inanimate objects human-like qualities. The listener may process these as a metaphor relating to themselves.

Maverick, your ego's writing cheques your body can't cash.

The chairs you are sitting in have heard this stuff so often that they know the content better than me.

That's the happy chair, don't sit in it unless you are going to smile.

Of course, I don't know if they think I'm joking or being truthful, but it gets a smile. Apparently, Milton Erikson used to say, "That's the 'Trance Chair'; don't sit in it unless you want to go into a trance."

Utilisation — using what the person says, or, in hypnosis, the sound of distant traffic.

I know you are not ready to go ahead yet because...
Any sounds in the background will help you to relax more and more...

I put the following example together for an NLP training programme that I ran for the sales managers of a major washroom suppler.

The scenario involves a sales person in a meeting with the facilities buyer for a motorway service station. The person knows that service station management are trying to process coach-loads of customers through the toilets quickly, and then into the café to spend their money:

"I know you are wondering how we can help you. It is important to have quick drying equipment. All the best operators are moving towards this technology and it means you'll give a better service, doesn't it?"

I know you are wondering (mind read) how we can help you. It is important to have quick drying equipment (lost performative). All the best operators are moving towards this technology (universal quantifier) and it means (complex equivalent) you'll give a better (comparative deletion) service, doesn't it (tag question)?

Remember, Milton Erikson did not use these labels, he just talked and that *means* you can too (complex equivalence)!

The 'Yes' Set

The aim of this is to move people to accept the suggestion you are making, possibly to give them confidence about something they are about to undertake. The idea is to get them nodding in agreement with you whilst you make them believe they can do something. This is very useful for teachers and personal trainers!

Start with several guesses pacing their experiences.

Here is what I taught support workers of a city council, who work with young people leaving care, to practice:

> 1. I know you struggled to find work at first.
> 2. But you are doing well in your job and getting great experience.
> 3. You can see you have grown over the last year. And that means that you are ready for a new challenge, aren't you?

See if you can write one for your own area of work or home life.

Linguistic Assumptions

This topic area is useful in three ways: as we have previously said, how would you like to read between the lines of something someone was saying and work out whether they thought they had no choices, in other words, that they are below the line? This could be one of your team or a coachee. You will develop the ability to really listen to what they may mean. The concept of transformational grammar suggests that the words used by someone are at the surface but they represented a meaning from the 'deeper structure' of their model of reality or their script.

By paying attention to the words they use at the surface, you may get a clue about their 'deeper meaning'.

The same applies when someone uses metaphors to describe a situation. They are representing their internal belief system and reality through the metaphor. This is useful because you can develop a meaningful conversation to explore their reality and challenge their thinking, which is, of course, the role of an excellent coach.

We are also going to suggest questions you can respond with to change their take on the situation and re-frame it for them. Any question you ask which changes their internal representation for the better is a result!

Finally, how do you know that you have not made a guess about what they mean, in other words, you distorted it. See the example below about running out of money. If a 'word' is mentioned in the coachee's sentence, it is a linguistic assumption and, therefore, you can conclude that is what they are saying, if not, you could be guessing and distorting what they mean. For example, one of your team states that they have "run out of money this month". You may assume that they want a pay rise, but when you question them to clarify, they explain they have paid for their holiday and it was their partner's birthday. Pay rise is not mentioned in the sentence. In coaching it is important not to second-guess what your coachee means.

The linguistic assumptions were given the following labels by John Grinder and Richard Bandler, some are repeated in the Milton and meta models:

1.**Existence**—a person, object or subject, e.g., a webpage. (It will be a noun.)
Example: *I'm a slow learner.* Challenge: *When are you not slow?*

Let's use another example; a manager phones the HR contact centre and says, "I don't know how to get the holiday approval form off the intranet."

The HR person replies, "Ignore the first paragraph on the intranet and download the form."

They will get an Internal Representation of the right place on the web page because the HR person used a negative by telling them to ignore it. Which gives the illusion of the manager having less to do.

2. **Possibility/Necessity** — (have to, must do, got to, can't and won't are modal operators of necessity.) They indicate lack of choice and that the coachee or team member may be below the line, and not buying into what the leader is proposing. We discussed in the meta model section that we can limit ourselves by forgetting that we have a choice and that, by realising that we have chosen to be where we are in life (mostly), then that can empower us.

You can respond with clever language to nudge them along by changing some can'ts to cans.
I can't do this.
I know you don't think you can, but could you consider the possibility that you might be able to, you can, can't you?

Tag question displaces resistance.

3. **Cause and Effect** — blaming someone or something else indicates being below the line. For example, they say, *I have too much on to complete the project on time.*

Ask a better question. *How could you do it? What are the barriers to completing it on time? How can you overcome each one?* These all create positive internal representations.

4.Complex Equivalence — (that means 'that' or 'because'.) As above, they are probably below the line. For example, *we have not got their order yet and that means we won't be able to despatch it in time.*
Response: *What can you do to find out what they require?*

5. **Awareness** — (these are visual, auditory, kinaesthetic verbs.) These can be used to soften and displace someone's resistance, e.g., *you may* notice *you can do it easily* after *you have been on it a few times.*

6. **Time** — (stop, now, after.) The coachee says, "I've *never* been able to do it, I *always* had a problem", indicates being below the line. You can use *after* as we have in the previous example to move their thinking to a time in the future. Past tense is useful, *old* is a good one as it puts things behind them, e.g., *What was that* old *problem you had?*

7. **Adverb/Adjective** — usually I use this rather than recognising it in the language of a coachee. An adverb or adjective can be used to soften what you are saying and to displace resistance; "you'll *notice* (awareness) how *easy* it is, *after* (time) you have had a go, won't you?"
Note, I have used several other linguistic tools here, e.g., *after* puts the listener in the mindset they would be in if they had already completed it!

8. **Exclusive/Inclusive or Double Bind** — this is useful in coaching, often people give themselves two options and you can ask, "what else can you do?" Or you can give them a double bind, e.g., "Would you like to do that this morning or in the afternoon?" It gives an illusion of choice!

116

9. **Ordinal** — a list.

I'm not sure if I should finish studying before I get a job.

Could you start applying while you are finishing your studies?

You can use this pattern to 'bury' what you want them to do.

The first thing you will notice when you exercise is how well you sleep at night.

Where are we going to celebrate after we hit our team targets?

This last one you can take away and use; it utilises time and changes the internal representation to after the event that was perceived to be difficult.

Other Language Patterns

In addition to the labels used in the linguistic assumptions, another one I like is the use of space. By this I mean: above, aside from and behind. Let me give you a few examples. These words join others in a sentence and by altering them you can change the coachee's internal representation:

I can't talk to her, she is too far above me. (Meaning salary grade). Response: *How many metres?* This loosens up their internal representation of the problem because they confuse seniority with a measure of distance.

I shake in front of my boss. Response: *What do you do behind him?* or *What do you shake?* Credit here to Mary and Wendy on a master practitioner course!

Another good set of questions, which loosen up their problem follows. It is important that they don't verbalise a

117

response, just have them think about it. If they speak, it does not have the same impact.

They say, *I have a problem with X*. Response: *Don't answer me, I'd just like you to consider this*, aside *from that, what else have you got?* You could also say, *don't answer me just consider, what else have you got besides the problem?*

We can also use negatives and 'nots' to loosen up someone's problem. For example, *I have a problem.* Response: *What is NOT the problem, just consider it, don't say anything.* They have to consider everything else they have, which is NOT the problem, e.g., resources they can use.

These all work by getting them out of their current internal representation which loosens up their internal barcode of the situation.

Chapter Fifteen — Rapport

You will rarely succeed without having rapport with people. If you want to achieve anything at work, or with customers and suppliers, good rapport is essential. It will give you an edge. We were doing an NLP workshop for a group of photocopier sales people. One chap said, "I am in a great mood when talking with my customers, but I give the order processing teams and credit control a hard time if they hold things up."

Another delegate, who was one of their region's top performers interjected, "That is why you are not selling as much as me. I'm best mates with everyone back in the office. If an order gets stuck or they are on stop I just give my colleague a call and usually the order gets approved and put to the top of their list."

I cannot think of any line of work that rapport does not impact on. Building relationships is key.

Rapport is a state we are in when we like someone, or we have something in common. For example, when I discover a delegate is a fan of F1 motor racing we have something in common to talk about.

If you ask any sales person or coach, they will emphasise the importance of being in rapport. Rapport is vital for everyone, whether you are a delivery driver or the managing director.

The following section includes techniques that will enable you to build better rapport.

Mirroring and Matching

When we are with people we like we often adopt a similar physiology. According to Daniel Goleman in his book *Social*

Intelligence we have 'mirror neurons' in our brain that make us want to unconsciously copy another person's physiology.

Mirroring is where you are standing or sitting opposite someone and you notice that you both have your legs crossed or you are both leaning the same way. Have you ever been in a coffee shop or a pub and noticed that you and your companion take a drink at the same time? A few years ago, I was having a coffee and I could see a couple at the other end of the cafe. He had his back to me and she was facing him. He had his head tilted to his left and she had her head tilted to her right. They stayed in this position for quite a long time. I bet they are holding hands, I thought, and when I went to pay, sure enough they were.

If you lean to your right and the other person leans to their left, that is called mirroring. Matching is where you both lean to your right or left and have a similar physiology to them with other body parts or positions. For example, if one person has their ankles crossed, the other person may sit with their hands crossed on their lap.

In NLP Practitioner training, and some body language training, people are taught to deliberately mirror the other person. I find that noticing a person mirroring me acts as a useful sign that we are in rapport and I rely on natural rapport. But, there is a danger when mirroring that the other person is aware of it and thinks you are doing it deliberately! This will break all rapport.

TIP — Be yourself, be a friend, take time to listen and get to know a person. Let them talk about themselves first.

Rapport through Language — Chunking Up and Chunking Down to Gain Rapport

We all have a level of language we are comfortable using. Senior people who operate strategically can have a tendency to use more abstract language and someone at an operational level may use more detail. How would you like to keep rapport with your managing director? Or, more importantly, how would you like not to lose rapport with your managing director? Chunking up is like a conversational executive summary.

Here are examples of both chunking up and chunking down.

Let's chunk up on car:

What is car an example of? Vehicle
What is vehicle an example of? Transport
What is transport an example of? Movement
What is movement and example of? Action
What is action an example of? Energy

And now we'll chunk down on car:

What type of car is it? A Ford Mondeo
Is it a petrol or diesel? A Diesel
What size engine is it? 2 Litre
What is the BHP? 150
What colour is it? Dark Grey
What age is it? One Year Old
Are the seats leather or cloth? Cloth
Is it a manual? Yes

A few years ago, an engineer informed me that he was attending the leadership-training course because he wanted to be promoted and become the manager of a business unit. His company hired out plant machinery. I could soon tell what the problem might be. He was so detailed! I taught the group how to chunk up and next time I saw him he said he had been practicing. Within four months he had received the promotion and I'm convinced it was because he learned how to gain rapport by chunking up. I imagine in previous interviews he might have been asked how he would improve the business. His response would have probably been, "I'd post inspect all equipment coming back to the depot and implement a rigorous planned maintenance scheme." The interviewer probably wanted to know how he would increase sales and develop new business.

People who are higher in auditory digital (we'll explain what that is later) tend to use a lot of detail when they are comfortable with you, and it is useful for them to learn to chunk up.

A good question to chunk yourself up is asking, *what is this an example of?* For example, "I went to St. Anne's junior school", would be, it's a place where young children are educated.

Use a question to politely chunk others up rather than "get to the point". How about, "What will the end result look like?" or, "What will that give us?"

Senior people have to be 'big picture' to manage large-scale operations and they operate at that level neurologically. A delegate on a programme informed me that the feedback in his appraisal was he needed to be more strategic. "Chunk up," I replied.

Chunked up questions are useful in both sales, "What is your biggest problem?" and in coaching, "What is your goal, or what would you like to achieve?"

We can then ask chunked down questions to understand their situation and get the detail we require. Also, chunked down questions uncover what they are deleting, generalising or distorting as they speak. Chunked down questions are just who, how, why, what and when questions. We used this process in the meta model.

Implementing Change

If senior people are generally abstract thinkers, imagine what can happen when they introduce transformational change. They may not consider all the detail, that is not their job. However, they can see synergy and similarities between business units or departments, whereas those at an operational level may see more differences, because their neurology is used to more detail. John Kotter identified a number of reasons why transformational change can fail. He discovered that there was infrequent communication about the change and that, whilst most people received lots of information on a daily basis, the major change initiative was only communicated a few times.

As leaders we can support change by communicating to staff that the detail will come later and by encouraging the senior team to communicate more frequently, even if there is no new development.

Our section on values levels will also explain why change can be resisted.

Negotiation

Imagine a difference of priorities between a factory manager and a sales manager. Neither sees the other's requirements as essential. They are both focusing on their own patch, neither one is seeing the bigger picture. This is because they are both operating at their own neurological levels. If we were to chunk up the factory manager and ask what their purpose was they may reply that it is to produce products to the production schedule efficiently and to the correct specification. If we ask them, what is the purpose of doing that, they may say it is to ensure the customer receives their product on time and is completely satisfied. If we asked for what purpose, they will say it results in more business and profit for the company. Now we can ask the sales manager what their purpose is, they will reply that it is to keep the customer satisfied, and we ask what is the purpose of that, and they say so that we get repeat business and that we make a profit.

Once we chunk up both parties, the lower level stuff seemed less important. In negotiation, chunking up both parties can result in a mutually beneficial conclusion. However, most people operate at a level they are used to, in other words, their neurology is highly developed at that level. You will have to take them up in stages.

Reframing

When we chunk up on a situation, for example, a disagreement or a setback, it can change our perspective. Let me give you an example. A trainer we know had four days of work cancelled at short notice and there was no cancellation agreement. She was very disappointed. I said to her, "Imagine you are looking down on your calendar for the whole year and see all the dates you have done for them last year and this year, how many are planned in."

"Quite a lot," she replied, "and my relationship with them is really good."

"A few days doesn't impact much then," I said. "And you've been telling me for months you did not have time to update your website and now you can."

Chunking up and down is really useful in business. For such a small concept, its application is vast.

Representation Systems and Rapport

Representation systems are a preference we have for using one or more senses. These are visual, auditory, kinaesthetic, our own internal dialogue and how we process information or self-talk.

Let me start this section off by saying that you probably won't recognise everyone's primary representation system/s, but that does not matter, because you're building rapport naturally and listening to what they are saying. Just relax, and if you notice a trend in the words they are using it's a bonus.

When Richard Bandler and John Grinder modelled Virginia Satir they discovered that she would gain rapport by using the words from the same representation systems that her clients were using. We have a tendency to represent our thoughts and internal world using words from our favoured representation systems.

Virginia, who counselled couples, would also translate from one client's representation system into the other's. For example, one partner might say, "I don't *feel* she loves me."

The other would say, "He doesn't *show* me how he loves me."

She would translate the kinaesthetic into the visual for the visual person and vice versa.

The words are sometimes called 'predicates'. Here is how we denote them.

Visual (V) something you see. Auditory, sometimes referred to as auditory tonal (AT), is something that someone else says or a sound. Kinaesthetic (K), a feeling, or tactile touch. Auditory Digital (AD), this is our self-talk and our internal processing, how we make sense of something.

V	AT	K	AD
Look	Hear	Feel	Make Sense
Shiny	In Tune	Grasp	Ticks the Boxes
Imagine	Clicking	Solid	Understand
Clear	Into Place	Concrete	Process

Have a go at translating these into another rep system; I'll start you off.

Today is going to be brilliant! (V)
Today feels great! (K)

Things are clicking into place. (AT)
It's making sense. (AD)

It's a solid proposal. (K)

The car looked beautiful. (V)

The words we use can give a clue to our favoured representational system or systems. For example, someone can be very visual and also high on auditory digital. This is known as the primary representation system. If we can detect someone's favoured representation system, we can build rapport by using similar language. Another clue can be in the level of detail. Those who are auditory digital may, when comfortable, use lots of detail in their language. If you asked them how they decided to buy their new television, they will tell you about the hours of research online and how it had several of the latest input connections and was a very high specification and that they shopped around for the best price.

A sales person on an NLP sales course with me discovered he was very high on kinaesthetic and very low on auditory digital. He remarked that he was potentially missing out on 20% of his customers. He learned to discuss more functionality and specifications to develop rapport with his customers who were higher on auditory digital.

We are going to learn how to put this information together with a person's eye movements and sometimes this will give us a clue to their favoured representational system.

Lead Representation System

A definition is where the eyes go first to discover information. It is their unconscious strategy for searching for information. The fact that it is unconscious still means that you can get into rapport by using words, that match their eye movement e.g. if they look up to their left or right a lot you can use words such as see, can you imagine, paint you a picture etc..

Have you ever been told to look someone in the eye because it's polite? Yet when you notice someone's eye movements they seem to move all over the place. However, if something is at the forefront of their mind their eyes will not move. They will move when they are searching for information or trying to construct something in their mind, such as a question to ask you.

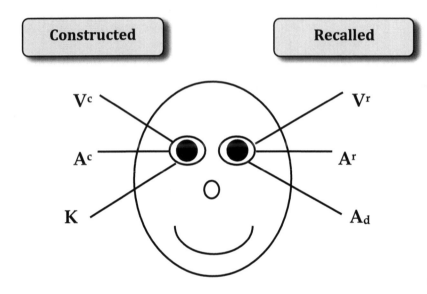

V^c = Visual Constructed
V^r = Visual Remembered
A^c = Auditory Constructed
A^r = Auditory Remembered
K = Kinesthetic (Feelings)
A^d = Auditory Digital (Self-Talk)

As you look at the person their eyes will look in a particular direction to gather information. This is the eye pattern chart for a 'normally' organised person. A small percentage of people are 'reverse' organised, so the visual recall, auditory recall and auditory digital are on the left as you look at the person, (their right). It is suggested that there may be a correlation with left-handedness, but this is not always the case. The best way to discover this is to ask questions that are deliberately kinaesthetic and deliberately auditory digital. For example, "What did it feel like when you first held (child's name) in your arms?" We would expect them to look down to their right to kinaesthetic if they were normally organised and down to their left if they were reversed.

Visual recall is where we go to access pictures or an event.

Auditory recall is where we go to access sounds or what someone else said.

Auditory digital is where we go when we are working something out or processing information. Auditory digital is our self-talk.

Kinaesthetic is where we are accessing feelings or thinking about someone we have feelings for.

Auditory construct is where our eyes go when we are constructing a sentence in our mind before we say it, or if we are imagining how something may sound.

Visual construct is where we go when we are constructing an image in our mind. People go to construct if they can't recall something. You may ask someone what the colour of their first school uniform was and they look up to their visual recall and don't get it, so their eyes move to their visual construct. You may hear people say that you can detect when people are lying because they go into visual construct. I don't believe this is necessarily true; they might not be able to 'get it' in recall so they go to construct.

Another reason for going up to their right may be because they are reversed organised. As we have said, this means that visual recall, auditory recall and auditory digital are on their right and visual construct, auditory construct and kinaesthetic are on their left.

Sometimes the eyes will go to different positions. If I was to ask you, "What did your first teacher's voice sound like?" Your eyes might go to auditory digital to make sense of what I had asked or repeat it back to yourself, then you might go to visual recall to get an image of her, then your eyes might move horizontally to auditory recall as you recall the sound of her voice.

There are three basic things to note:

When a person's eyes move the words (predicates) follow a second or so later which demonstrates a link between eye movement and the representational system words.

If a person is thinking about a loved one, they will probably look down into their kinaesthetic. Likewise, if they are asked the route they took in a car journey in France they may go into their auditory digital while they are processing. If we ask directed questions the eyes will be more likely to move to those positions.

For building rapport and getting into the other person's 'world' it is useful to ask open questions such as tell me about your last holiday and look for trends, i.e. do their eyes move up a lot to visual recall or construct, it does not matter which, it's just means they are visual. Or do their eyes move down to their kinaesthetic or auditory digital, or left to right horizontally? Do they use words from one or two representation systems frequently and do their eyes go there, too?

When you are coaching, you will be asking questions then listening. Your coachee will be doing most of the talking. This gives you the opportunity to sit opposite them and be aware of their physiology, eye movements and listen to see if you pick up any clues from their words. Sometimes you will pick things up and sometimes you won't. But when you do you can use it.

If you are in a selling situation and by selling I also mean where you deliver a service internally in your organisation, you are going to start by asking chunked up questions followed by chunked down questions to gain an understanding of their situation. Once again, they will be doing more of the talking and you will get the opportunity to pick up on words, eye movements and physiology, i.e. are they mirroring you?

A few years ago, I was with a potential new customer. Her eyes kept moving up to her visual construct as I looked at her. It does not matter if their eyes move to visual recall or to visual construct, if they are going to visual then they probably favour visual. I asked her if she was free the following Thursday, so we could *look* at their current training materials and *see* if we could add value to their programme. She nodded, and we got 36 days of training with them that year. She also did the representation test we use and came out high on visual. You can get a copy of the test if you contact our office.

At times we may come across people who don't move their eyes very much, so when we are communicating with them we have to rely on their words. Or they may be very visual and AD, but you see lots of visual eye movements, yet rarely see their eyes move down to their left. This is where you have to listen out for the 'process' words. The same goes when you are on the telephone. Read the following and work out what this person's preference or preferences are.

131

How did you decide to buy your last television?

Our area was getting the latest broadband technology from our provider and we were exceeding our old download limit, so I decided to go for the new fibre optic system, which included the TV latest packages. Our old TV would not show these in the best light, so I decided to use some of my bonus to buy a new TV. I had seen the new Samsung in a department store and thought it looked great. It had a large screen with a narrower frame than the Sony or other models. It just looked so much better! My wife suggested I checked out the price and I noticed that two other shops had the same TV for the same price, but a higher spec. I wanted to buy it straight away so that it would be installed before the engineer arrived with our new digital box and broadband. I went to the store. I looked at the displays and saw the Samsung; it still looked great! I checked with the sales person that it had all the functions I wanted and that they had it in stock. I bought it and it came with a free 5-year guarantee.

So, what did you pick up there? There are a lot of visual words and a lot of detail, indicating a person who processes a lot, i.e., auditory digital, there are also a lot of auditory digital words, too.

Let's look at the paragraph again with my comments.

How did you decide to buy your new television?

Our area was getting the latest broadband technology from our provider and we were exceeding our old download limit, so I decided to go for the new fibre optic system (AD), which included the TV latest packages (AD). Our old TV would not show (V) these in the best light (V), so I decided to use some of my bonus (AD, value for money and cost are clues to AD) to buy a new TV. I had seen (V) the new Samsung in a department store and thought it looked (V) great. It had a large (AD) screen with a narrower frame (V) than the Sony or other models. It just looked

132

(V) so much better! My wife suggested I checked out the price and I noticed (V) that two other shops had the same TV for the same price (AD), but a higher spec (AD). I wanted to buy it straight away so that it would be installed before the engineer arrived with our new digital box and broadband. I went to the store. I looked (V) at the displays (V) and saw (V) the Samsung; it still looked (V) great! I checked with the sales person that it had all the functions (AD) I wanted and that they had it in stock. I bought it and it came with a free 5-year guarantee (AD).

As we have said, people with a higher AD will often go into more detail. They often do a lot of research when deciding to buy and may get a discount.

The key to this additional information, eye movement and sensory-related words, is to be relaxed about it and build rapport with a person by being genuinely interested in them, then you will notice some or all of these things and you can use them to assist your communication.

Chapter Sixteen — Values

How would you like to be able to motivate anyone in your team or find out what motivates your coachee? How would you like to help your team members to get more job satisfaction and fulfilment? I'm guessing that if I asked you these questions you would say a big, fat YES.

Why are values an important topic to discuss? Do you set goals and sometimes not achieve them? Do you sometimes seem to be working really hard, but you are not getting the financial rewards you desire? Are you getting fulfilment in your career?

Our values operate as one of our filters. They are often deeply unconscious. We act in accordance with our values without being consciously aware that it is a value that is driving the action. Values make up a big part of our script.

Our values create motivation to do something. For example, someone who exercises will probably have health pretty high up their list.

Values are what we move away from or what we move towards. Values are things we are willing to spend resources and time on.

Where do values come from? The first source is family, your parents, how they acted and what they taught you. What were their values as you were growing up? Next are your teachers and school friends, what they did and how it influenced you. This will continue through school, further education and employment.

Economics can play a big part in the formation of your values. Young people starting their careers during a time of low unemployment are probably more confident of work and jobs being plentiful, so are less likely to have security in their top values.

Morris Massey suggested that all values are formed during the major periods. From ages 0-7 is the imprint period, where we soak up our values and beliefs, from 8-13 is the modelling period, where we have our heroes: a favourite footballer or singer, and 14-21 is the socialisation period, where we learn to mix in groups and form relationships. Morris Massey implies values don't change. However, from an NLP point of view that does not fit, because it is all about change, and events such as having children can change values. The values levels described later also support this argument. A good film about values changing featured Tom Cruise in *Jerry Maguire*.

We can elicit values about our life, or in business we can elicit career values, which could overlap with life values, i.e. family life and work—life balance may appear in your career hierarchy. For me, happiness incorporates both these things.

We hold our values in a hierarchy; often we are not aware of some of those that are important to us because they are held within our unconscious.

The problem occurs when there is incongruity and conflict among the values in a values hierarchy. A typical career-values hierarchy may look like this:

Success
Being seen to do a good job
Being liked by my team
Money
Independence
Respect
Happiness
Enjoyment

Before we look at the values listed, I want to discuss the concept of 'toward' and 'away from' values. Taking an extreme example, if you asked a woman, "Why did you marry your husband?"

And she replied, "Because he does not do drugs and does not drink excessively," those values are 'away from' what she does not want. However, if she had replied, "Because we have similar interests and I love spending time with him." That would be 'toward.'

Another example might be a self-employed coach who feels uncomfortable when their diary is not reasonably full for the next three months. They may even book work in as an associate of a larger company to put dates into their diary several months in advance so that they can see it filling up! The feeling they experience of being uncomfortable when their diary is not particularly full is a signal of an 'away from'. An empty diary, at its lowest level, relates to no money in the bank and a lack of security. However, the energy this 'away from' requires could be spent on prospecting better clients.

Being seen to do a good job could be an 'away from' because it infers a need for an external reference to *doing a good job*, rather than an internal frame of reference that *you know you are doing a good job*. The same applies to *being liked by my manager* and, possibly, some aspects of *money* could relate to security. 'Away froms' use up energy, sometimes through anxiety, and change our focus from our goal. The coachee usually recognises an 'away from' themselves because they get a negative feeling when they become aware of it.

'Away froms' would constitute a conflict between what you want and what you don't want. In the example hierarchy, *being seen to do a good job,* may indicate a need for approval, which in turn may prevent a person challenging their manager regarding something the manager has asked

137

them to do in a specific way. There may be a better way, but the employee does not want to offend their manager (this is all happening unconsciously), because, if they do, they might not be considered for that promotion that may come up in two years' time. This is in conflict with value number one, *success*. If a person feels uncomfortable challenging, they possibly won't be as effective. Likewise, the coach who is filling their diary as an associate, possibly on a much lower day- or hourly-rate is 'being busy', so not seeking out customers for themselves and earning half what they could if they were working directly with their customer.

'Away from' values will cause internal conflict between working toward your goals and limiting or satisfying the 'away from'. Because you will be trying to fulfil the 'away froms', it will use up energy, potentially creating stress and reducing your ability to achieve goals. There is a strong link between 'away from' values and limiting beliefs. Using the submodality limiting belief change, we can cause a shift in the 'away from' and with Time Line Therapy® we can remove the 'away from' values completely or change their meaning, so that they become totally towards. A good example of this is the value of *money*, which may be mainly 'toward' but contain a percentage of 'away from'. Once we remove the limiting belief, the value of money may remain in the values hierarchy, but 'feel' different, in a more positive manner. We will use the example of money to discover how we identify 'away froms'.

The first step is to discover and prioritise our values, then determine if there are any that contain a proportion of 'away from'. An 'away from' is usually only a percentage of a value. For example, money could be both about having a comfortable lifestyle and security.

Values can relate to any aspect of your life: career, relationship, children, recreation, and health, etc.

TIP—The most effective way to elicit values is to elicit someone else's and in turn they can elicit yours. The reason for this approach is that we have to ask the same repetitive question to elicit a long list, possibly of 30 or more, to enable you to get to the unconscious values. If the other person is writing them down for you and asking questions, your focus is not taken away, so you are forced to search more deeply and recover those held within your unconscious. Don't be tempted to discuss what the values mean, otherwise you will be distracted from the task. There will be plenty of time for that when you start coaching around achievement of the values.

Before we start, let me remind you of what we can achieve by using this process. You will know exactly what your individual team members are motivated by and you can coach them to increase their fulfilment of those values in their current role and career. You will have a highly motivated team of people each with a plan to fulfil their values.

The Process

Let's call the person eliciting the values, the coach, and the person whose values you are eliciting, the coachee.

Step One
You are going to write down all their (coachee) values on one side of a piece of A4 paper, so that they are able to prioritise them. We ask four different questions which will allow as many values as possible to come out. Because we

are eliciting career values, we ask, "What is important to you about your career?" Not their current role, as they may not be happy in this. They will answer and possibly pause. We then keep repeating the question. "What else is important about your career?" We just write down the words or phrases they use. We do not have to get clarification. They know what they mean. You will probably get a list of about 20 values or more, it may take 15 or 20 minutes. You are looking for several long pauses during this first step, so you know that they are getting the unconscious values.

We then go to question 2.

"Think of a time in your career when you were really motivated (say it with feeling), go back to that time, see what you saw, hear what you heard and tell me the feelings." They will list several, such as energised, in control, excitement, and we add these to our list.

Next, we go to question 3 and ask, "If you had all these, (point to their list) totally satisfied in your career currently, or in your current role. What would another opportunity have to offer to make you want to take it?" (I never say job, I keep it vague.) And they might say, "More freedom."

We add that to our list and ask the fourth question which is, "Well, we don't want you to leave, so we can offer you 'more freedom' too. But what else would we have to offer you in addition to that to make you want to stay?" And they may say "security," which we add to our list.

We then have a list that we give to them to prioritise. It is important that they use all their responses from the four questions and number each one to make one list. If two words come out twice, count it as one number. When they have finished you may have something that looks like this:

6) Money

18) Being in a team
19) Local
7) Work—life balance
9) Friendship
21) Being seen to do a good job
10) Company car and benefits
22) Travel
15) Working in different places
17) Autonomy
5) Being respected
25) Enjoyment and happiness
11) Solving problems
23) Being developed
12) Developing others
8) Achievement
24) Doing a good job
13) Praise from my manager
4) Recognition
2) Career path
14) An organization that has values
16) Energised
20) Powerful
1) Success
26) More Freedom
3) Security

Now we have this example completed, note that some of the higher values were elicited further down the list and the number '3' —career value of *security*, was from question 4.

1) Success
2) Career path

3) Security
4) Recognition
5) Being respected
6) Money
7) Work—life balance
8) Achievement

The top eight are the main drivers. However, we give consideration to all the values by numbering them. And qualified master practitioners of NLP can change values in the hierarchy. For example, if the coachee wanted number 17, *autonomy*, to become a more important value the master practitioner could do that. They would never change a coachee's number 1 value!

However, following a limiting belief change using Time Line Therapy®, the 'away from' values would be removed, and other values could take their place in the hierarchy. As a leader, knowing that a team member has a partial 'away from', you can discuss it with them and, between you, minimise its impact by giving them support and confidence.

Motivation

When encouraging a team member, you may unconsciously motivate someone with your own values. I remember a sales manager asking me what he could do to get his sales people to attend team meetings.

"Are meetings important to the sales team?" I asked.

"They should be," he responded.

"Why?" I replied.

"Because they are," he said.

Working as a team was very high up in his values hierarchy, but these sales people could earn 120% of their salaries in bonuses, and may not see how team meetings could have an impact on their income.

Theories of motivation, such as Maslow's hierarchy of needs and Herzberg's 'satisfiers' and 'motivators' are too generic to offer much value to the individual coach or leader. That said, the more you can reduce the impact of poorly perceived company policies, the better. As we have demonstrated, values can be held unconsciously, so it is only the more conscious values that might be discussed using the Herzberg model.

I remember being told by several 'management trainers' that money is not a motivator. They went on to say that it is only if you discover that someone in a similar position is earning more than you that money becomes important. However, I would suggest that money can be very important for some people. Other values, such as success, may result in you earning more, without money necessarily featuring in the top eight values.

We can use a person's top eight to coach them around each value in order for them to satisfy more of the value in their current role, or identify the next steps in their career path.

We'll use the example from our previous elicitation. In this process the coach or leader will use the coaching style with the employee/coachee. Remember, the coachee has to be above the line and the actions they take have to be their idea. I would still use the same approach if I were their line manager, giving them responsibility for their career development.

1) Success

2) Career path
3) Security
4) Recognition
5) Being respected
6) Money
7) Work—life balance
8) Achievement

Take success first.

The coach would ask: "As a rough percentage, to what extent is success being fulfilled in your current role?"

The coachee responds, "60%."

The coach asks, "What does success mean to you, what does it look like or feel like, what is happening?"

Coachee: "It feels good, I feel happy, I'm helping people and getting results."

Coach, "Okay, let's go back to that fulfilment of 60% for the value of success, what can you do to increase that?"

Coachee thinks about it and says, "I would like more responsibility."

Coach: "How can you gain more responsibility?"

Coachee thinks for a while and suggests that they could project manage the forthcoming new contract.

Coach: "What would that lead to?"

Coachee: "It would demonstrate that I was ready for a contract manager's job, so that if one came up in the group I could apply for it."

Coach: "Is there any other area that you would need to develop to fulfil the competency requirements for that position?"

Coachee: "I would like to work on my delegating skills, but I think I can develop that by project managing the new contract."

The coach and coachee then discuss how this could be managed, what sort of support and coaching would be required, etc.

This is an abbreviated conversation. In reality it may take longer. The coaching activity is then repeated with the other seven values.

We teach this on our leadership and coaching programmes and delegates love it. The proactive leaders use it around appraisals or as a follow on to appraisals, or just as part of a one-to-one. One senior accountant recently told the other delegates in the group that half of his team were very motivated and engaged. When asked about the others, he replied, "I have not done the career values and coaching with them yet, but once I have they will be!"

Our qualified coaches use it with their coachee as a tool to support them in achieving their goals and to achieve greater job satisfaction.

You might ask: what about the people who don't seem interested in a career? For some, a career is not even in their hierarchy of life values, or at least not in the top eight! Money may be the reason they go to work. If you want to elicit a coachee's life values, just repeat the exercise above asking, "What's important to you about life?"

You can use your values rather like a compass to set the direction for your life. They will assist with your decision-making and will ensure that your career follows your purpose.

Identifying 'Away From' Values

1) Success
2) Career path
3) Security

4) Recognition
5) Being respected
6) Money
7) Work—life balance
8) Achievement

The benefit of identifying 'away from' values, or values with a percentage of 'away from', means that we can be aware as a leader that our team member has an 'away from', and, therefore, may not challenge us or other influential people. They may have a better idea or way of achieving the result we want. As the leader we can reassure our team member that we are open to their ideas and, as a team member, we can question our first reactions to something and reflect on why we are not questioning the way we are being asked to do something, especially if we have a smarter solution.

An 'away from' around *security* may result in the team member or coachee being risk averse. I recently had a delegate on a leadership programme who felt that he was more secure in his current role than if he developed himself and sought promotion.

"If you develop yourself, won't you be more attractive to employers and more marketable?" I questioned.

"I had not seen it like that and it still feels daunting, but more doable now." He responded. "Maybe this course will help me with my confidence," he grinned.

The Process

As with the values elicitation exercise, you need to do this with someone else. It is important to be listening out for them saying should, must do, and have to. And if they

146

respond to your questions and get a negative feeling, then it is probably an 'away from'.

Let's use the example of value number 5, *being respected*.

Coach: "Why is being respected important to you?"

Coachee may respond: "Because I like people to think *I'm good at what I do.*"

The coach asks, "Does that feel like a 'toward' or 'away'?"

Coachee: "It feels like a bit of an 'away' because I have a feeling of fear in my stomach.'

At this point the coach can either ask again, "Why is being respected important to you?", or they could follow up on the coachee's previous response and ask, "Why is it important *that others think you are good at what you do?"*

This one could go either way.

They might respond with something like, "If others do not value what I do I might not get promoted."

Coach asks, "Is that a 'toward' or an 'away'?"

Coachee responds, "It feels like an 'away'.'"

After we have asked why the particular value is important to them three or four times, we ask, as an approximation, what percentage is the value a toward or away. And they may say 40%.

We may chart it out like this:

1) Success	T T T	100% Toward
2) Career path	T T T	100% Toward
3) Security	T A A A	50% Away
4) Recognition	T T A	30% Away
5) Being respected	A T A	10% Away
6) Money	T A	10% Away

| 7) Work — life balance | TTT | 100% Toward |
| 8) Achievement | TTT | 100% Toward |

Coaching With 'Away Froms'

Most, if not all, 'away froms' stem from a lower level limiting belief. If you have access to an NLP practitioner who is trained in Time Line Therapy®, you could refer your coachee or team member to them. Two city councils we work with have all their internal coaches trained in NLP and Time Line Therapy®. However, that may not be possible, so now we are going to show you how to coach the person on their 'away froms'.

We'll use number 5, *being respected*, as an example again. We have established that they believe *"If others do not value what I do I might not get promoted"*. Let's start with that.

The Coach asks, "Do you know when you are doing a good job yourself?"

Coachee: "Yes."

Coach: "Every time you do something, and you evaluate it, can you tell if you have done a good job?"

Coachee: "Definitely, but I like confirmation from my manager and the director."

Coach: "Do you think that your manager is aware that you like confirmation that you are doing a good job?"

Coachee: "Probably not."

Coach: "On the occasions you don't get any praise, do you think your manager might have other important tasks to be getting on with and may not even be thinking about your area of responsibility?"

Coachee: "That's true, and he would let me know if he was not happy with something."

148

Coach: "Would you say that your own evaluation of your ability is the same as your manager?"

Coachee: "Yes."

Coach: "And your evaluation of your own worth, is that the same as your manager and the director?"

Coachee: "It probably is, in fact, I don't know why I have been letting it bother me. I know I do a great job."

Coach: "What are you going to do in the future?"

Coachee: "Focus on my objectives with the full confidence that I have his support."

Values coaching, and teaching values, is one of my favourite subject areas because it can enrich individuals and create energy within teams.

Chapter Seventeen – Apply Clare Graves' Value to Leadership, Coaching and Your Results!

In the 1970s, Graves proposed that people, countries and organisations could be at different neurological values levels. Chris Cowan and Don Black have developed this work over the years and written a book about their findings, *Spiral Dynamics*.

The concept of values levels provides insight into change management. For example, if an organisation is predominantly values level four, then change will be resisted. By understanding the dominant values levels, you will be able to affect larger change and take people with you. These values levels are also depicted in colours, but I find numbers easier to work with.

There is not necessarily one better value, some may be more appropriate in different environments. Most people span across several levels, e.g., someone could be a little bit of 4 and a dominant level 5, with some level 6 and a little 7.

Graves suggested that people can 'think' at a higher values level than their neurological development. There are methods we can use to test which values thinking a person is at, but one can only observe the neurological level by their behaviour. So, someone's thinking may be a five, but their neurology still has some three. When their position is threatened at work they may revert to aggression.

Let's explore the different levels:

Values Level 1

This is about survival – at this level, people's neurology has not developed sufficiently to do anything else. Often a person who is seriously ill can go back to values level one.

At values level one the focus is on the individual. Their dominant drivers are feeding, fighting, fleeing and er...

Values Level 2
"Self-sacrifice to the way of your elders," is the way Chris Cowan and Don Black describe level two. It started around 40,000 years ago with the development of tribes. Values level two is focused on the group, rather than the individual. There is no separation between subject and object and there can be magical beliefs and superstition. Level two is about rituals and rites, (even footballers wear lucky socks or touch the ground when they come onto the pitch). Children talk to teddy, and teddy is real! There are parts of the world where people are still at level two. In areas of North Africa, some people will have some level two neurology and thinking. One could argue that some of the individuals leading them are at values level three.

Values Level 3
The focus is on the individual. They want total control for their personal survival and gain. They may become the tribal leader. Typical examples are the Mafia Don and Rambo. The level three beats all others to the ground, or at least goes down in glory. They will respect other, more powerful, level threes. The Wild West is a good example of values level three. Children go through level three, it is sometimes called 'the terrible twos'. It is also noticeable in some teenagers. They need the structure and discipline of a level four environment to progress and develop their neurology.

Values Level 4

The transition might go like this. The values level three can't go on fighting and realises there is more to life. The theme for level four is self-sacrifice now, in order to receive in the future. Law and order replace chaos. A good metaphor for the transition from level three to four is that the outlaw may become the sheriff.

Level four is about the rulebook, the church and organised religion, in fact, anything with a rulebook. In business, the quality management standard ISO 9001 and Health and Safety legislation are very much about values level four. The term, 'non-conformity', is pure transactional management behaviour.

Many organisations operate or operated at level four; a 'job for life', a good pension. However, this was combined with a know your place attitude and rewarded with a gold watch for longevity of service. Loyalty is rewarded, life is predictable and secure. There are 'proper' ways of doing things. People at values level four can also be very judgemental about others. "Oh, look at her dirty windows!" You will often hear them putting others down, noticing the same faults in others that they display themselves. The same trait applies to level six too.

We can see level four being required in traffic laws and for personal safety. In organisations, it has a management feel to it, rather than transformational leadership. Many public and, to a degree, private sector organisations operate at level four with some level five. Government departments love to cascade targets into the NHS and schools. They are well-meaning, but are typical of level four neurology. They can lead to management of efficiencies rather than the organisation being effective. Staff and managers become demoralised by the approach and can forget their original vocation.

Some organisations apply rigorous procedures to ensure health and safety legislation is applied, which is a positive level four approach. Whilst good safety and health processes protect people, sometimes when management applies level four thinking to customer service, it can stifle creativity and excellent service. For example, often customer service is taught in good faith by head office to multisite operations, and measures are put in place to monitor adherence. Examples of these are: *Would you like a bag for life?* or *We answer all our calls in four rings.* Mystery shoppers are employed to monitor the implementation of these standards and local management are measured on their adherence to breeding more 'norms'.

I remember the speaker, Richard Gerver, telling a story about being a little peckish at the airport. Seeing white baps and sausages he asked for a sausage bap.

"Sorry, sir," replied the person on the counter, "sausages are only with the English breakfast options."

"Yes, but I don't want the full breakfast," Richard responded.

"Well, sorry, sir, we are not allowed to serve sausage sandwiches, we have not got a price on the till."

"Okay," said Richard, "I'll have the full English without the bacon, egg and beans, oh, can I buy a bap too?"

"Certainly, sir," replied the young man behind the counter.

I was talking to an ex-bank manager the other day. I asked him why he had left the bank and he responded by saying, "Steve, every evening I had to telephone my manager and report on 19 separate measures."

As we have discussed, excess level four behaviour reflects a management approach that will stifle employees' ownership, they won't take risks, they have probably stopped making suggestions and their energy levels on a scale of one to ten are probably as low as two!

For many people who want independence, this environment can become frustrating, their thinking becomes level five, but they have not taken action yet to develop their neurology.

When you start coaching and developing someone who is a dominant at level four, they can transcend to level five. There is a possibility that they will start to focus on less important issues; it is important to keep them focused on results. They may also have an underlying anxiety and fear that they are not aware of, but you can be, and support them accordingly. The goals and objectives need to be in small steps and they should be tasks they can do on their own to develop independence.

Values Level 5
Values level five is about the need for individuality and for what they want for themselves, but not at the expense of others, like at values level three. People operating at this level can still be self-centred and insensitive. They believe that things can change and that they can influence it. In the film *Jerry Maguire*, Tom Cruise's character is all about money. The person at predominately level five is not prepared to wait for the hierarchy to retire before gaining promotion, their attitude is, "I want the gold watch now!" Though it is usually in the form of a BMW or Mercedes these days.

How do you spot a values level five? Things to look out for: designer watches and suits. They want to find out about themselves, they will be keen to do the Myers Briggs test, etc. They will have a 'can do' attitude and be entrepreneurial.

As I have said, the thing about all these values is that people can think at a certain values level, e.g., level five, but have not fully developed the neurology to operate within a new environment, which holds them back. True level fives may be employed or self-employed and will want for themselves. Many people finding about NLP are values five or six and want to move to level seven when they discover what it is.

In coaching at level five there will not be many negative emotions but they may have a need for security and some limiting beliefs, so NLP techniques are useful.

Values Level 6

As the neurology of level five develops, they may start looking for more from life and search outside themselves for more meaning. They may take an interest in human rights, the environment and the wider community.

Level six can be a little judgmental about others, even their friends.

They sometimes find it difficult to take action. They may enjoy meditation. They will love Reiki and hypnosis; it may even have helped a level five to move through to six thinking. The 1960s (love not war, "peace, man" and all that) saw a lot of people move to level six, but then they shaved their beards and put on a suit and went back to level five to earn a living.

When coaching people at level six they need to agree to goals that will stretch them, and complete them on their own. They should monitor negative feelings towards others, and not criticise other people's behaviours because they are just a reflection of their own (development area) faults.

Values Level 7

Values level seven cares for themselves, but never at the expense of others and in a manner that all life will profit. They are good at handling complex issues. They are very pragmatic, functional and effective. They can achieve a lot in a short space of time.

They will take action when concerned for others or the planet.

It is said that they represent a small percentage of the population (at a neurological level). They are trustworthy, open and honest. They are unlikely to focus on negative thinking for long, if at all. They show flexibility in a stressful environment (because their neurology is developed to handle it).

If they are uncomfortable in an organisation they will try to change it to a win-win practical solution. If this does not work, they will leave. It is unlikely you will need to coach a level seven, you will be more likely to coach a five or six, with level seven thinking but not level seven neurology. That said, someone at level seven could be coached to help them set goals and have an even bigger impact.

Remember people can be at several different levels in their neurology and their thinking. In tests they will operate at level four and five, with level six thinking. Alternatively, someone may operate at level five with level six and seven thinking. People go back to their neurological levels when the environment is stressful.

The level seven is a transformational leader. They see the best in people and can bring it out of them. They inspire, they get results seemingly effortlessly, but they work very hard. They are extremely effective in getting a lot done without the 'baggage' of a four, five or six.

Values levels can be seen in different aspects of life and may help explain the behaviours you see in others. It is encouraging that there does seem to be a development in values levels across the planet, though there have been setbacks in the Middle East. The USA displays several values when you look at the country simplistically, Florida a solid four, complete with the death penalty; New York, five/six; and California a six.

See if you can spot the dominant values levels of people around you.

Chapter Eighteen — Goal Setting and Achievement

"Twenty years from now, you will be more disappointed by the things that you didn't do than by the ones you did do, so throw off the bowlines, sail away from safe harbour, catch the trade winds in your sails. Explore, dream, discover." — Mark Twain

Back to The Future

Marty McFly comes from a dysfunctional family; his dad is bullied by Biff, an old school enemy. His mother is a bit over weight and smokes like a train. Then he gets whisked back 30 years in a DeLorean Time Machine created by his buddy, Doc. Once back in 1955, he has to make his parents fall in love to ensure his own survival. But his dad George is an utter wimp, famous for one-liners, such as, "you are my density". Marty sets his own mother up in a parked car and plans for George to save her. Unfortunately, Biff comes along and attempts to assault her. George stumbles on them and finds a 'new belief and confidence', knocking Biff to the ground with an Ali like left hook, he rescues his future wife. However, later at the 'Enchanted Ball', some dude tries to step in and dance with her, at first, he capitulates, then realises his new-found self-belief!

Marty eventually gets back to the present and awakes to find his family life completely changed. His brother is wearing a suit, his mum and dad look fit, healthy and confident. His dad, George, has a book published and, outside, Biff is waxing Marty's new pick-up truck. The tables had turned, George was the confident one with a great life!

And that brings me nicely to the point. Your past was created a long time ago and has resulted in where you are in life right now, only you don't have to go back in a DeLorean Time Machine to change it. Where you are today is more important, the past is the past. Your memories are probably distortions of what happened. What you create in your mind today will become the seeds of your future, even if you are 80 years old.

One of our delegates, Kim, told us that her favourite saying is, "A ship may be safe in the harbour, but that is not what it was built for." And, anyway, when it's not moving through water, the barnacles gather on the vessel.

Okay, we know the ship should be sailing somewhere, but to which destination? The crew set the exact coordinates of the port into the navigation system, rather than letting it drift aimlessly. The same applies to us and that is why it is important to have a purpose and set goals.

The Goal Setting Process

I have been using a goal setting process for 20 years. Over time, I have wondered why some goals worked out with a fantastic result, while others seemed unachievable, and others fell by the wayside. I have drawn some conclusions, which I will share with you.

There have been many books written on goal setting from *Think and Grow Rich* by Napoleon Hill to *You Can Have What You Want* by Michael Neill. They share common themes that seem to have been passed down over the last 150 years or so. My first experience of a goal setting process came from Lou Tice and involved writing affirmations, self-talk and trusting in your filters (Doorman) to open up with information.

In this chapter I am not advocating a goal setting methodology or stating that you can have everything in life that you want, so don't rush off to the Bentley dealership!

What I am proposing are simple techniques that I use, which are based on the NLP goal setting process.

My own observations of successful goal achievers include that they work extremely hard. They focus on a task, they work effectively and efficiently, they do not procrastinate and they will often do the least favourable task first so that they are not thinking about it all day.

TIP – "If you have to swallow a frog don't look at the sucker all day." Zig Ziglar

I set about using the methodology in Lou Tice's *Investment In Excellence* programme. The first major achievement I experienced occurred whilst investigating the cause of a quality problem we had. Electro-mechanical components were being rejected by our customer because of contamination; it was only ten in a million, but we wanted it to be zero! This problem had been with us for a while and, following a reorganisation, the issue was given to me to solve. Buzzing with enthusiasm from my course I wrote a goal out as if we had achieved it already. (See the process, which follows.)

I had written my goal on a little card and read it every day, after a few weeks, I noticed I was talking with people about it and gathering information – my 'Doorman' was at work! On one occasion it was with someone outside of work, whose company had access to technology that could identify extremely small particles, such as the particles contaminating the product. A few weeks later the production manager in the factory identified two potential root causes.

I want to go through a few steps in goal setting and we will discuss what works and when it does not, and the possible reasons why. Before we start, there are two schools of thought regarding setting goals. The first is that it should be time-bound, in other words, we set a date when we want it to happen. The other view is not to set a date, because it could take longer, or may even happen sooner. I do both, depending on what the goal is.

In summary here are the steps:

1. Have a strong desire for the goal.
2. Be totally committed, you have to decide to do it.
3. Make it specific and visualise it as if already achieved.
4. Have a certainty and belief that you will achieve it.
5. Expect obstacles to come up.
6. Take action, and put in lots of energy.

Have a Strong Desire and DECIDE to do it!

I would quite like a Porsche 911. They look nice, particularly in blue, like my friend, Gareth's. Paul around the corner has bought the new Carrera S. However, there are only two seats and we are a family of three, plus a black Cocker Spaniel. A Porsche would be nice, but I have no emotional desire to have one. Whereas, when I selected my last four-seat Audi, I was eating, breathing and sleeping it.

It is vital to have goals that excite us and create emotion and motivation. I discovered that if I am really passionate about something, then I put more energy into achieving it. Think carefully, draw up a wish list and then discard what you don't really want, don't dispense with something because you have doubts about achieving it though, we'll come to that in a moment.

162

It is a good idea to have balance and set a few goals in different areas of your life. Once you have several, maybe a few short-term, 90 days or so, medium-term, up to one year, and long-term, three years or more, you can write them down on your notes page on your phone or tablet, where you can look at them at least daily. I'll show you how to write out your goal in a minute.

Then DECIDE to do it. I found that with all my goals that were successful I had made a conscious decision to do it.

Have Confidence in Your Doorman

We know that our doorman and filters open up to information when something is important to us. We can set more stretching goals in the knowledge that when we start working towards them information will be all around us. In fact, what I do is make notes under my goals when things happen which demonstrate progress towards the goal. It is not always obvious what is happening; yes, you will find yourself talking with people, reading new information and noticing people who are doing similar things. Some of what may be happening will be under your conscious radar, it may only be when you look back over a few weeks or months that you will notice a pattern of things occurring.

How to Write Out Your Goals Correctly

The human mind cannot hold two different pictures of the same thing without creating tension. If you scratch your nice, shiny car you will have a strong urge to get it repaired as soon as possible, because that's the picture in your mind of how it should look. When you view a new house and the bathroom is not as appealing as the one in your current home you may say, "This is the first thing we'll do when we move in." But if you don't get the scratch repaired, then after a while you will hardly notice it. The desire to get the car repaired will reduce over time. Likewise, with the bathroom, if the refurbishment gets put off, it won't happen. This tension is called 'creative tension' or 'cognitive dissonance'. Essentially our brains can't hold two different pictures of the same thing. Imagine an elastic band held between your thumbs, one hand above the other. The elastic band creates a force to bring your thumbs together. Your brain operates in the same way.

If we write a goal specifying exactly what we want, in the first person, as if it is already completed, then the same creative tension will form in our brain. We can read and visualise that goal several times a day. The key is in the detail, using words that trigger emotion and pictures of what we want.

Examples:

Suppose you are a size fourteen or a waist 36" and you want to lose weight, here is how to write a goal. You can embellish it as much as you like with lots of emotional words.

I look great in the mirror in my size 12 blue dress/my new jeans. The gym was hard at first, but I soon got into the habit of going.

We achieved our stretching sales target of 20% (you can put more specific numbers in) for the last financial year and are celebrating tonight with the whole team in Piccolinos.

It is graduation day, looking back three years ago, when I enrolled, it seems like a lifetime ago. I am just walking on to the stage to receive my scroll from the assistant dean. Flash goes the camera!

164

Have Certainty and Belief

I realised a few years ago that the goals that did not come to fruition were those which I did not really have a strong desire for, or where I lacked commitment or complete certainty that I could achieve them. As a result, I only put in a half-hearted effort.

We can do something which will increase our certainty. We do this on training courses when we teach goal setting. It's called the 'Certainty Game'.

Think of a goal that you are not certain you can achieve. If it were five, six or seven out of ten, for example, I would ask you, "How certain were you that when you came back from lunch there would be chairs in the room?"

And you would reply, "Ten."

"Now, how certain are you that you can achieve your goal?"

And you would say, "Seven, eight or nine."

"Now, once again, how certain are you there would be chairs still in the room?"

"Ten," you would reply.

"Hold onto that feeling. How certain are you, that you can achieve your goal?"

"Ten," you reply.

You can do the same thing in your home, i.e. "How certain were you when you walked into your home there would be chairs in the lounge?"

It works because we keep the same internal representation from the certainty of the chairs. It is what is known as a submodality technique, which we will explore later.

165

Expect an Obstacle — Have Total Commitment

It is essential to have commitment. Unless you are committed, you have not set the goal, it is almost like *deciding* that you are going to do it. Many people don't fully commit to a goal because they have doubts about achieving it. But, if you are committed, then when the obstacles come up you will be ready for them. In fact, once you have written out your goal, identify the obstacles you can foresee for each one and develop a set of actions in your 90-day plan to overcome them. (We'll do 90-day planning soon).

Never Leave the Game Before the Final Whistle

Last Sunday afternoon, I took Josh to watch Aston Villa play Tottenham Hotspur. We had seen Villa beat Man City a few weeks before, so we were looking forward to the game. We only live half an hour from the ground, but after the match it can take up to an hour to cover the first two miles before the traffic is clear.

Villa were playing well, but were 2-0 down, 15 minutes to go! We were excited! Villa mounted attack after attack. With five minutes to go the family next to us vacated their seats. As the clocked ticked into the four minutes of extra time whole rows emptied in a rush to leave the area. As we got into the last few seconds around 10,000 people left the ground before the final whistle.

I read an article recently by Ian McCurrach, in which one of his top tips for success was: "Never leave the game early, never give in – tough times don't last, tough people do."

For the sake of a bit of traffic, those supporters made it pretty clear to their players that they did not believe they were going to win, never mind equalise!

When we set and achieve goals we are almost certainly going to face obstacles. People who get results know this, and they may even welcome the obstacle because it shows them they are on the way. As soon as we even think about the possibility of failure our whole mindset changes and we become less certain of a successful outcome, this results in changes to our behaviour and less energy and effort being applied. Don't leave before the final whistle.

Take Action

This morning, before getting down to writing, I decided to mow the grass. Our old motor mower has been great over the years. I just push it along and it cuts the grass very quickly. It needs petrol, of course, and requires several pulls on the starting rope before the motor growls into life. Sometimes it takes more effort than others. It is a little like a metaphor for the goal setting process, our unconscious mind is a goal setter, opening our mind to new information and coming up with creative ideas, but before it kicks in we need to do some hard work.

Taking action is vital; you can't just call on the universe and expect stuff to happen. A good place to start is to list an action plan that will move you towards each goal. Then plan time in your diary to complete those tasks. In a moment I'm going to take you through a 90-day planning exercise, but, first of all, I would like to show you an activity we use in coaching to help people achieve their objectives and become more effective. You can use the same process with your team, looking at their individual areas of responsibility.

Becoming More Effective

I do this when the coachee believes that they are not doing as well with their objectives as they would like, or they are not being as effective as they could be. That said, this is a useful exercise for anyone to do and I review mine every few months.

I start off by asking them what they are employed for and they give me the usual corporate waffle with bits from their job description. I reply, "No, what is your output, what is the result of what you do?"

If they are a sales manager they might reply, "I ensure my team is developing new leads in our target customer sectors and exceeding budget with our current customer base."

If we focus on our *output*, not what we do, it helps clarify our thinking. Maybe habitually we are working hard, but doing some of the wrong things.

Next, I get them to use an A4 piece of paper and write 'big impact' at the top and 'little impact' halfway down. Then I ask them to list all the big impact things they have been doing over the last few months and all the little impact stuff that gets in their way.

Example using the sales manager:

Big Impact – 50%
Testing new methods of marketing and promotion
Developing sales team to increase their lead generation
Accompanying sales people on customer visits
Looking after my own key accounts
Delegating administration
Developing sales training with supplier
My own CPD
Improving sales processes with internal departments

Little Impact – 50%
IT issues
Customer complaints
Attending some meetings
Chasing orders from production and operations
Investigating payments with credit control
Performance management
Re-doing things that could have been done right first time

We have our list and we go through it, first though, I ask them for an approximate percentage of time they spend in each section. The figure I've shown of 50% is typical. Next, we look at the little impact activities and try to establish the root causes and potential solutions to reduce or stop doing the activity using coaching. We would not, for example, want to delegate more little impact stuff without first finding ways of improving the process.

We then review the big impact list. Firstly, I would question why the manager of a large sales team has their own accounts, surely this could be delegated? A few years ago, I worked with a sales manager who was 30/70. Six weeks later he had delegated all his accounts and done more accompaniments with team members (coaching) than in the last five years. He was also getting home earlier and spending more time with his family.

Then, we look at which of the 'big impact' items we could give more of our focus to, for example, making the sales process with internal departments more effective. These objectives would be fed into our 90-day plan and diaries for action. However, what if something is missing from the big impact list? In other words, you don't know what you don't know. Your current big impact list is based on your current thinking and model of the world. This is where modelling comes in. You could ask yourself is anyone in a different sector or organisation getting better results than you in a similar field? If so, what is their thinking and what are they doing differently to you, or you could be coached to facilitate your own thinking.

90-Day Planning

I am a big fan of 90-day planning. This involves deciding and listing the most important things we can do in the next 90 days and making time in your diary to achieve them. It is a simple process and does not pressure you to do everything this month, however, it does allow a reasonable time to plan the activities which move us towards goal achievement. This can easily be done as a team exercise too, enabling you to allocate projects to team members.

Taking action is essential to goal achievement. We normally start off well in January, putting events in the diary, creating space to get things done, but then something crops up and we get busy and it's Christmas again. But what if we give ourselves a break and just plan for the next three months? Rather than doing everything straight away, or setting plans for a whole year (which means we will keep putting things off), we commit to doing our action plan in 90 days. I take a page from my notepad, fold the page in half, a trick I learned from Mark, and write my list in the two columns. It gives me space to list 12 or so actions. I may develop a more detailed plan for each action on a separate page. I then allocate times and dates in my diary for when I'm going to do something towards them.

I was in the dentist waiting room this morning and picked up Esquire magazine. The article that I chose was about Paul McCartney.

He was asked by the interviewer: "Clearly, you don't need the money, and you don't need the fame, so what are you doing here playing a series of concerts in Japan, when you could be at home with your feet up?"

To which McCartney replied: "Two reasons: I love it and it's my job..."

"You've never seriously contemplated retirement?"

McCartney responded, "Sit at home and watch telly? That's what people do, man. Gardening, golf... no thanks."

The point is that we need to have purpose and goals, even at 73! I find it an inspiration that someone of his age is still touring, on stage for nearly three hours a night and writing the best songs he has done in twenty years. But it is not just about being inspired, it's about taking action too.

Chapter Nineteen — NLP: The Techniques

In this section, I am going to show you techniques which NLP practitioners use with their clients. Some I have adapted so that you can perform them on yourself.

Anchoring

How would you like to feel confident or calm in any situation? For example, do you ever get a little nervous or need a boost before an interview or a presentation? We are going to give you a 'super booster button'. Otherwise known as a 'resource anchor'.

Let's look at how it works, this technique is something you can very easily do yourself. Anchoring occurs when a neural connection is 'linked' to a highly intensive state.

It is based on the work of Pavlov who famously rang a bell and gave his dogs steak, as expected, they salivated. He repeated the process a number of times and then just rang the bell (no steak!) and they still salivated, the noise causing them to anticipate the food.

Before I tell you how to set up an anchor that will help you access a positive state, we'll talk about anchors generally.

A few years ago, we were visiting my parents. Whilst in the kitchen I noticed a small round red dot stuck on a cabinet. Later, I spotted another sticker on the landing. "What are those red dots for?" I asked my mum.

"Oh, they remind me to stand up straight." (She has back problems.) Her trigger was a red dot. We use pink dots in some of our workshops to remind delegates to be their 'better selves'. Some stick them on phones and others on their laptop screen. One woman told me it was going on her husband's forehead!

Positive states can occur when you hear a favourite song on the radio or smell a perfume or look at a holiday photo.

Resource Anchor

How would you like to be able to press the knuckle on your left-hand forefinger and go into a positive, confident state? As I said, you could use this before a presentation, an interview or a meeting.

We use a knuckle because it is easier to replicate the position. There are three ways we can install positive states:

1. As a positive state is occurring, e.g., as you graduate, win new business, you are congratulated at work or your favourite team has just won a match.

2. By recalling a time when you were in a highly intensive positive state.

3. By changing your physiology to what it would be if you were highly motivated, for example. (Note, this should only be used when you cannot recall a time you were in a specific positive state.)

Let's explore the first one. Any time that you feel really good press firmly on the knuckle of your left-hand index finger with the index finger of your right hand for about 15 seconds. (The opposite if you are left-handed.) This will stack positive states. You can carry on adding to it whenever you are feeling really good, energised, motivated, etc. When you need to access the good state, just press on your knuckle until you go into the positive state.

The second way is to recall an event when you were in a positive state. Good states include: motivated, powerful, happy, resourceful and confident. Pick the ones that give you the strongest feeling.

Go back to that time, see what you saw, hear what you heard and feel the feelings of being in this positive state. As you enter the state, apply your finger quite firmly onto your knuckle and hold it for 10-15 seconds at the peak of the feeling. Repeat this 5 or 6 times with several states, choosing the strongest memory; it's okay to repeat the best ones for you. Examples of good states to apply are:

Totally motivated	Energized
Confident	Laughing
Powerful	Exhilarated
Excited	Euphoric

After you have done this, 'break your state' by working out what seven times eight is, then test your knuckle by pressing on it. You will go into a really good state. Any time you want to add to it you can, by either using this method, or the method above, in other words when you are in a naturally very positive state. This is the method we teach new coaches on NLP practitioner training so that they can do it with their coachee.

The third way is used where people cannot recall a time when they were motivated. You can use this third way to get into a good state using your physiology and self-talk. Stand how you would stand if you were really feeling strong, confident, shoulders back! Now adjust your breathing until you feel motivated and press your knuckle.

Personally, I prefer methods one and two, although I've used method three at conferences.

Barcode for the Brain

Let me tell you something, the following concepts are the best-kept secrets in the world!

At the age of seventeen you were probably not taught how to get rid of your limiting beliefs so that you could become more confident in your exams. What if your teacher could have done a technique with you to give you the confidence to go for a higher grade? Remember, we don't set the goal unless we believe we can achieve it.

Submodalities are how we encode our reality. Rather like an internal barcode, they give meaning to our memories and what we perceive. Submodalities are the constituent parts of the modalities, which are visual, auditory and kinaesthetic senses.

If I went into the supermarket to buy a bottle of reasonably priced wine and when I scanned it the till read £120.00, I would think something was wrong, particularly as I had expected it to be much less than that. I would take it to customer services and they would provide the correct price. On investigation they may discover a fault in the label manufacturing resulted in an incorrect barcode being attached to the bottle.

My suggestion is that you may have some *faulty barcodes*.

So, the truth, as you see it, may not be the truth, your reality is based upon the information you have deleted generalised and distorted. All coded. And, of course, you read the code and it dictates your thoughts and feelings. If your barcode for speaking French was rated as poor, then that is your starting point. Let me give you an example. Suppose you like coaching your team but not doing performance management. Each part of your job will have its own bar code, and will dictate whether you feel comfortable doing each task. I'm not saying we are going to enable you to like doing performance management, but what would happen if we took the bar code you have for doing performance management and made it the same as the barcode you have for raising your expenses, or another innocuous task?

Limiting beliefs have a barcode too. In a little while, I'm going to show you a variation on a simple technique to reduce or remove a limiting belief.

Back to submodalities or how we encode and give meaning to events or beliefs. Here is a list of useful ones:

Visual
Black and white or colour?
Is the picture in black and white or colour?

Near or Far?
How close is the picture to your eyes?

Bright or Dim?
Is it bright or dim?

Location?
Is it left or right from central, or up or down?

Size of the picture?
Full screen, the size of a TV, A4 or smaller?

Associated / Dissociated?
If you see yourself in the picture it is dissociated, if you see it through your own eyes it is associated.

Focused or Defocused?
Is it clear?

Focus changing or steady?
Is the view changing or focused?

Framed or Panoramic?
Is the picture framed or not?

Moving or Still?
Running as a movie?

Auditory
Can you hear any sounds?
If yes, what are they?

Location
Of the sound, maybe coming from the picture.

Direction
Where is the sound coming from?

Internal or External?
Is the sound external or in your head?

Loud or Soft
Is it loud or quiet?

Kinaesthetic — *What are you feeling?*
Location
Of the feeling in your body.
Size
It could be filling their chest.
Shape
They might say it is round.
Intensity
On a scale of one to ten?

Submodalities are used by NLP practitioners to remove or reduce limiting beliefs; to remove phobias; to help a person be confident in specific situations and to enable them to complete tasks that they do not like doing. These tasks can then be completed without a second thought, in other words, they now feel neutral about doing them. These are but a few uses for submodalities; there are other uses too.

According to Richard Bandler, a university decided to advertise for people with phobias to discover how they got them. Richard went for a completely different approach, he advertised for research subjects who once had a phobia but had got rid of it on their own. He discovered that, in each case, when they ran the movie of their fearful event, e.g. the first time they were frightened by a spider, they had 'stepped out' of the picture and were seeing themselves in it, like watching yourself on a TV monitor. We call this 'dissociated'. Where we see a picture with our own eyes but are not in it, we call that 'associated.'

When looking at our internal representations it's worth picking something good! Close your eyes and go back and remember an enjoyable holiday. Have you got a picture?

Okay, it's not going to be as vivid as your Samsung TV, but have you got a picture? Good!

Is it black and white or colour?
Is it near or far?
Is it bright or dim?
Is the location up or down from eye level, or left, or right?
What size is the picture?
Do you see the picture through your own eyes (associated) or do you see yourself in it (dissociated)?

What feelings are there? You will probably have good happy and relaxed feelings.

Bring the picture back up and make it black and dark, the size of a postage stamp and blast the picture 1000 metres away from you until it's a tiny dot. Now, where are the feelings? They have probably gone, so bring the picture right back in front of your nose, make it big and bright.

Okay, you might say, "What is the point of taking my good feelings away?"

We can do it with negative emotion too, such as anger. Suppose you have an altercation with a colleague. Go back to the time of the event, or the worst event. Close your eyes, do you have a picture? Check on the emotion of anger, is it still strong? Do you see them in the picture? If you are looking through your own eyes, change the picture so that you can see the picture with both of you in it. Make it small and dark and blast it 1000 metres away so that it is just a tiny black dot. On opening your eyes, you should feel neutral about the person. Now you can deal with them in a more objective manner.

You can do submodality change with other people too. A few years ago, a woman on a workshop said that as soon as her phone rang and the name of a person who reported to her came up she felt irritated. A few moments before, she had been laughing about her favourite cartoon character. I asked, "Could you put that character's picture in your phone with her number?" No sooner had I said this, she started laughing and could not get the 'old' negative feeling back. The current set of submodalities can be shifted by making something seem ridiculous. It can change a whole 'take' on a person or event or task.

Limiting Belief

Usually you would do this technique with a qualified NLP practitioner, which takes about 20 minutes, but let's have a play! I have set out a similar process for you to have a go at, it's not exactly the same as you would do with a qualified practitioner but may have an impact on your confidence.

Think of a limiting belief, such as, "I don't believe I can earn 'x' a year." If you don't believe you can earn 'x' a year there will usually be a lower level limiting belief underneath that. Really go for it and use whichever gives you the most uncomfortable feeling, "I don't believe in myself" or "I'm not good enough", are typically the lowest. Remember, these are deeply unconscious, so you may not be aware of them. Just go for the lowest one you can recognise. I have simplified the process so that you can at least make some shift for yourself.

Step 1. When you think of that (limiting belief) do you have a picture? Note, what comes up may be a metaphor for the limiting belief, whatever comes up, go with it. Close your eyes.

So, you have a picture, maybe it's to your left, or down, it might be hazy and not have much colour, possibly you see yourself in it. Remember, the picture might be an unconscious, metaphorical image that represents the limiting belief. Now, take the picture and change the location, if it is in front of you or to your right, move it over to your left at 45 degrees to your body and make it stay there. If it is to your left, move it to the right, open your eyes.

Step 2. Now, we want a belief that you are absolutely *certain* about, such as, "somewhere in the world the sun is going to come up tomorrow". Close your eyes and when you think of that do you have a picture?

It is probably in front of you and you are seeing it through your own eyes, it is possibly slightly above eye level and central, filling the whole screen.

Step 3. Now, think of the opposite of your 'old' limiting belief, what new belief do you want to have? You may say, "I totally believe in myself". Close your eyes and when you think of that new belief, do you have a picture and a set of feelings, possibly with some sounds?

Okay, whatever the picture is, make the submodalities the same as for the sun coming up, so you keep your new picture but make it the same brightness, location and see it through your own eyes, if that's the way it was with the sun coming up. Make the feelings the same, and as intense. Now seal the picture.

We can use submodality change for a number of things. It is the basis for getting rid of phobias. You can also swap a task you don't like doing, such as performance management, into the set of submodalities for a task you take in your stride, such as attending a meeting, which will take any apprehension you have away.

Location is a key driver, so is changing the picture from associated, (seeing the picture through your own eyes) to dissociated, (seeing yourself in the picture). I find just changing location has an impact.

Swish Pattern

You can do this by yourself. It is used for a highly contextualised subject, such as, "When I meet a group of people I don't know I feel nervous", or "When putting at golf I feel nervous".

Let's take the first example:

Step 1.
What is the problem?
When I meet a group of people I don't know I feel nervous.
When you think of that, do you have a picture?
Yes.
We'll call that the 'old' picture.

Step 2.
How would you like to feel or act instead?
Confident, self-assured.
When you think of that, do you have a picture?
Yes.
Make it so that you can see the picture through your own eyes. Adjust visual intensity, colour and picture size for the most positive feeling.

Step 3.

Step out of the picture, so you see your own body and shrink it down to the lower left-hand side of the screen in the corner. Open your eyes!

Step 4.

Close your eyes, take the old picture and bring it up on the screen? Make sure you are looking through your own eyes whilst being aware of the new picture, small and dark in the lower left-hand corner of the screen.

Step 5.

Now, very fast, have new the picture explode, big and bright, and have it grow so that it covers the old picture.

Step 6.

Clear the screen and open your eyes.

Step 7.

Repeat steps 4, 5, and 6 until you can't get the old picture up.

Finally, we would test how we felt about the old problem and imagine how we would feel in the future should a similar situation arise.

Perceptual Positions

"Before you criticize a man, walk a mile in his shoes. That way, when you do criticize him, you'll be a mile away and still have his shoes." Steve Martin

Perceptual Positions enables individuals and teams to 'walk in the shoes' of another and understand their perspective, and to take action to resolve problems and promote practical solutions.

This is a good technique to use as a leader or coach to improve the way people and teams relate to each other. But the person you are doing it with has to be above the line.

There are three positions:

Position A is the person you are working with.

Position B is the person who has a different perspective to your coachee or team member.

Position C is a fly on the wall looking at them both.

Sit your coachee in chair A and sit in chair B, the person they disagree with or have a difference in perspective. Ask them to tell you what is wrong. Get as much out as you can.

Next, swap seats, so you are the coachee and they are the other person. Ask them to tell you what is wrong with person A's perspective. Get them to point at you (it helps, trust me), and say *you* not *I* (third person language). You may hear things like: "you never listen", or "you don't understand that we have other customers to prioritise".

Once finished, they will already be learning from the situation.

Now get them to sit in position C, as far away in the room as is practical, and get them to comment on what is happening again using third person language. They can only comment on what they can do because the other person is not there, and your coachee/team member is the one who takes the action.

You can do this with your whole team if there is a problem with relationships with other teams, customers or suppliers. Mark out the positions on the floor and get them to stand in the relevant positions.

Chapter Twenty — Inside-Out

"And, in the end, the love you take is equal to the love you make."
The Beatles

I was with a quality assurance director recently who wanted to engage his workforce so that they would make fewer errors in production and improve product quality. He also told me that he wanted them to take more personal responsibility for their work and feel empowered. We talked about this for a while and we both agreed that it was about them feeling safe, so that they would not feel daft about expressing their ideas and that they should feel trusted.

"Do you trust them?" I enquired.

"Absolutely," he replied.

"Do they feel trusted?" I asked.

"Well, I think so," he said.

"Tell me, do you trust your office staff?" I asked him.

"Definitely," he responded.

Then I asked, "do your office staff clock on?"

"Certainly not, we trust them to manage their own work," he replied.

"What about in the factory?" I asked.

"They clock on," he said looking at his shoes.

This seemed to imply that even though his organisation wanted to empower their people, their values and belief systems were probably preventing the goal from happening.

We shall return to the concept of inside-out thinking; just to remind you, outside-in thinking is where we believe external events make us feel happy or unhappy, whereas with inside-out thinking, we know that it is our *thoughts* that make us feel happiness or gloom. As our thinking changes and awareness grows, we can begin to influence our reality. In chapter twelve I gave you the example of the elevator, which represents our levels of awareness or consciousness. At the lower levels, we see disagreements and negative emotions, but as we go higher up in the lift we are aware of other perspectives and our own negative feelings dissolve. Syd Banks suggested that, as we go even higher, the landscape becomes more of what we create from our own thoughts and subsequent actions. As our awareness and self-belief develop, our filters will allow us to notice new information and opportunities that we may have missed. In other words, our thoughts can create a new reality depending on the glasses we decide to put on. Remember the story about the woman who changed her approach to her teenage daughter? Her daughter responded differently and she created a new reality for herself. Remember, your 'Corrie' glasses will muddle your thinking creating fear and negative thoughts. Your NLP glasses will create clarity and calm, allowing you to access and follow your gut feeling or inner wisdom.

Your top eight values will provide you with a compass by which you can fulfil your purpose. As you develop your goals to achieve fulfilment of your top eight career values you can put plans into action. Along your journey you may face challenges. I sometimes experience a conflict between my head telling me I should do something but my heart telling me something else feels right and that is the path I follow. In my experience you will know what *feels right* and that can be your guidance system for progression and fulfilment.

Epilogue

A dark shadow emerged from the time machine. The shadow furtively glanced down the corridor. He plucked up courage and made his way towards what looked like a canteen, only much classier, no Formica tables or chairs with fag burns decorating the seats. The room was softly lit, with a few sofas and brightly-coloured tables and chairs arranged in a welcoming manner.

"Can I help?" enquired a young man with an apron around his neck.

"Er, who are you?" stammered Norman.

"I'm the barista," replied the young man, "would you like a coffee?"

"You don't look like a lawyer to me," said Norm.

"Oh," the young man laughed, "no, not a barrister. I serve delicious coffee, here, help yourself."

Norm reached for a number 6.

"You can't smoke in here," exclaimed the young man, looking at Norm like he had just defecated on the floor. He continued, "smoking is against the law inside public buildings. Surely you know that, no one does it anymore."

"Oh," replied Norm, "sorry, I'll just sit here and drink my coffee... Mmm, very nice," he slurped. Norm glanced around and noticed a few books and magazines placed casually on coffee tables. He picked up a magazine, glancing at the pictures of men dressed in suits but with no ties, and others wearing jeans with open neck shirts, some carrying leather bags and wearing woollen scarves. The prices were astronomical, £600 for a suit! He flipped through a few more pages containing adverts for other products, some that he had not seen before, he could only describe them as like small televisions. He came across an article entitled *How to be a Better You!* He began to read.

Later, he looked out of the window in the corridor. As he walked, he saw the passing traffic, the cars were, in the main, larger and bulkier than his. Eventually he came back to the room he had exited earlier. Quickly, he reset the dial to his own time and, with a judder and a shake, he was back outside his factory. As he reached his car he threw his cigarettes into the nearest bin.

He entered the front door of his house on the new estate at the edge of the town.

"I'm home, Brenda!" he called to his wife.

"Hello, my love!" she replied. "What has happened to your hair… it looks quite nice."

"Oh, I've been to the barbers, and I've got a new suit in the car. Anyway, you get dressed, I'm taking you out to that posh new Italian on the high street."

Monday morning came. Norm decided to walk around the floor beaming like he had just won the pools. Every so often he would chat and enquire about someone's weekend and about their kids.

Later, he called the team on the GEC job to come into his office for an update.

"It is really important we get it out on time," he smiled, "and I want to look at it myself before it goes to despatch, only the best quality leaves from now on."

They looked stunned, gone was Norm's greasy hair, instead it was cut in a more fashionable style. The suit had been replaced with dark grey and he wore a plain navy tie.

A few months later, he was called to the general manager's office. Jim 'Ginger' McCadden greeted him with a firm handshake and lit his eighth cigarette of the day. "Morning Norman, I don't know what is happening down there, but, for the first time in years, it looks like we are going to meet our production schedule and people are actually smiling! Not only that, attendance is looking better too! What on earth are you doing, Norm?"

"Just doing my job, Jim," replied Norm, with a grin.

Special thanks to Andy Cope for upping my game as a writer and for feedback such as *"Were you behind the bike sheds when punctuation was being taught?"* Also to Lionel, Laura, Barry and Dino from i2i and Polly Stretton for her original edit. Thanks to Tad and Adriana James for their teachings on values and NLP.

Recommended Reading and Listening

I would like to share with you some of the audios and books I have enjoyed, dip in and continue on your journey.

Zig Ziglar – *Strategies for Success* audio. Zig gives some excellent insights into how to develop yourself personally and professionally; his southern humour and anecdotes are very funny and his messages very powerful.

Steve McDermott – *How to be a complete and utter failure in life, work and everything.* Steve's recording is hilarious, and an absolute must to play in your car. Steve's stand-up style puts NLP across the way it should be.

Richard Wilkin's *Broadband Consciousness* programme compliments NLP and gives a great understanding of your script. Richard has a very down-to-earth approach keeping his messages very simple.

Paul McGee's *SUMO* is an excellent book and one we recommend to delegates on all our programmes. *SUMO* is about building resilience and taking personal responsibility but also allows for a little Hippo time.

Simon Sinek - *Leaders Eat Last* is a little meatier and provides some great insights into leadership. A very compelling read bringing the topic of leadership bang up to date. Have a listen to his TED talks too. Start with *Why* and *Why Good Leaders Make You Feel Safe*.

There are two books by Jamie Smart, which I found personally very useful: *Clarity* and *Results*. Jamie builds on the work of Syd Banks and explains the Three Principles philosophy with great clarity, I sometimes found myself thinking. I knew that but now I understand it.

Be Brilliant Every Day by Andy Cope and Andy Whittaker, *Quantum Physics Mansfield style* and so much more! The two Andy's take you on a journey showing you that happiness is here now, not at the end of the rainbow.

The Little Book of Emotional Intelligence by Andy Cope. A no nonsense, very funny approach to becoming happier and more emotionally intelligent. Andy is so much cleverer than many academics who research emotional intelligence because he has applied it himself and can teach you to do the same.

Steve Kay lives in Ashby de la Zouch with his wife, Dawn, their son, Josh, and Cocker Spaniel, Smudge.

Steve and Josh enjoy watching football together and are both learning to play golf.

Steve leads a team of trainers who deliver leadership and coaching training and their 'How to Be a Better You' workshops across the private and public sectors, enabling people to learn how to inspire themselves.

Steve also delivers the NLP Practitioner and Master Practitioner-certified training across the UK.

Follow Steve on twitter @SteveKaynlp
Or email Steve at stevek@qualityculture.co.uk

Websites   www.qualityculture.co.uk
                  www.nlpuktraining.com

If you would like to know more about our training please contact us. info@qualityculture.co.uk